'Give Me Arthur'

An advertisement printed in Alfred Shaw's biography in 1902.

'Give Me Arthur'

A Biography of Arthur Shrewsbury

Peter Wynne-Thomas

Arthur Barker Limited   London

A subsidiary of Weidenfeld (Publishers) Limited

Published in Great Britain by
Arthur Barker Limited
91 Clapham High Street
London SW4 7TA

ISBN 0 213 16925 8

Printed in Great Britain by
Butler & Tanner Ltd
Frome and London

Contents

Foreword by Derek Randall

By a curious coincidence, both Arthur Shrewsbury and I have visited Australia four times to play Test cricket, and to stretch the coincidence we both played thirteen Test matches in Australia – records, I understand, to be unequalled by any other Notts-born cricketers.

Reading this account of Arthur's cricketing travels, brings home to me how different were the conditions for players a hundred years ago – the long, monotonous sea voyage, the coastal steamers and the horse-drawn transport in the days before the railways were fully developed. Jet lag may be a problem, but it is preferable to the days of burning heat in the Red Sea and sickness in the Bay of Biscay, let alone cholera in Naples.

My tours of Australia have been full of happy memories and I have made a host of friends 'Down Under' – judging from his letters, Arthur also found Australia a congenial country, and the friendships he developed there, remained with him throughout his life.

The Australians have, of course, played many historic matches on my home ground, Trent Bridge. I remember in particular the famous victory Notts inflicted on the touring side of 1980 – unfortunately, going in at number three, I only made a dozen out of the county's total of 465. Arthur played in the very first match ever staged by the Australians in England – it was at Trent Bridge and Notts won by an innings and plenty, but Arthur, also at number three, made very little contribution to the score.

Cricket is for me, though, more than bare facts and records. It is more than a mere job, it is, as it must have been for

Arthur Shrewsbury, a way of life. Spending so much of my time at Trent Bridge, I have become conscious of the many batsmen who have preceded me down the pavilion steps and out on to the sunlit turf. The cricketers of long ago are not forgotten, and it gives me much pleasure to be allowed to introduce this biography of one of England and Nottinghamshire's greatest batsmen.

Derek Randall
June 1985

Preface

The remark 'Give me Arthur', made by W. G. Grace, has
become part of cricket's folklore. It seems to have been first
written down by 'A Country Vicar' (Rev R. L. Hodgson) in an
essay printed in *The Cricketer* magazine in the 1920s and then
transferred to Hodgson's book 'Cricket Memories', published
in 1930. In this version W. G. Grace was asked with whom
he would most prefer to open England's batting. By the time
the two romantic historians, Neville Cardus and G. D. Marti-
neau, used the phrase, 'Give me Arthur' had come to mean
that, barring himself, Grace regarded Arthur Shrewsbury as
the greatest of batsmen.

The precise origin of the comment is however of little sig-
nificance, for a study of contemporary newspapers quickly
reveals that the comment is based on fact, since journalists
and fellow players were in general agreement that, for about
two decades, Shrewsbury was England's outstanding batsman.

In view of this it is surprising that no biography of this
famous cricketer has ever been published. Apart from one or
two obscure pamphlets, the only work devoted to Shrewsbury
is W. F. Grundy's 1907 'Memento of Arthur Shrewsbury and
Alfred Shaw, Cricketers', a small book which mainly com-
prises obituary notices and similar tributes.

A chance meeting with Mr Gerald Shrewsbury, the great-
nephew of Arthur, revealed that the Shrewsbury family still
possessed some 300 letters written by Arthur and further
correspondence addressed to him. The family were kind
enough to allow me to study these documents and the result
is this present volume, which shows that Arthur Shrewsbury

was much more than an excellent batsman – indeed cricket was only part of his very active life.

From nothing he built up a thriving sports goods manufacturing and retail business, producing many types of sports equipment from cricket bats and tennis rackets to boxing gloves and footballs. He was the driving force behind four cricket tours to Australia, one of which was the first round-the-world tour by English cricketers, and he also managed the first English Rugby Union football tour. His other business interests were in the lace trade, in which he was a partner in the family lace firm.

Arthur Shrewsbury and his brother William both made their debuts in first-class cricket in 1875. At the time William was thought to be the better, but Arthur possessed the gift of patience and that, allied to his innate ability, produced the first of the great modern professional batsmen. Shrewsbury, it seems to me, must have realised as a teenager that he had the necessary gifts to be a good batsman, and by sheer unremitting practice in the nets and in local matches, set about developing that talent until he became the most complete batsman in England, if not the world. Before Shrewsbury came on the scene, batsmen, whether professional or amateur, allowed their natural aptitude to determine the standard of their cricket. Shrewsbury was not satisfied to let nature take its course. He developed batsmanship in the same way that modern athletes have used the science of training in the recent Olympics.

Shrewsbury showed the way, and many of the batsmen who followed him were, consciously or not, his disciples, the most obvious example of the present time being Geoff Boycott.

The game of cricket owes much to Arthur Shrewsbury and I am pleased to have been given the opportunity to write this book as a tribute to him.

PETER WYNNE-THOMAS
Haughton Mill, Retford
February 1985

Acknowledgements

May I express my thanks to those who have assisted in the writing and publication of this work, first and foremost to Gerald Shrewsbury for permission to use family letters and pictures and to Mrs Sybil Pollard, Mrs Doris Shrewsbury, Mrs Irene Sunderland, Mrs L. J. Plackett and Mr Donald Chapman, who are also members of the Shrewsbury family; and to Keith Warsop, Philip Bailey, Philip Thorn, Stephen Best, David Stapleton, Hugh Aixill, Roy Spiller, Malcolm Brown of the Queen's Hotel, Stuart Wharton of James Shipstone & Sons Ltd, Martin Corteel and Peter Arnold for their advice and help on specific details.

1 From Lace to the County Team

18 December

Self Bowled by A. Attewell when not looking.
W. Marshall bowled by self if bails had been on, but stumped same ball.
W. Marshall clean bowled by Gunn.
Self clean bowled Henson.
Present: A. Shrewsbury, Henson, Marshall, J. Gunn, A. Attewell.
Neddy was present but did not play.
Dark day, light very bad.

This is the first entry in the only extant diary of Arthur Shrewsbury. The details, in a plain hard-backed pocket notebook, run from 18 December 1900 to 29 March 1902. Recorded are the days on which Shrewsbury went to the indoor nets at Trent Bridge – nothing more. Entries occur every three or four days for the months from December to March.

It is understandable, perhaps desirable, that a young cricketer should keep a careful note of his performances in the nets. In 1900 however Shrewsbury was no tyro. He had completed twenty-six years of first-class cricket. All his youthful contemporaries had long since quit the rigours of three-day county cricket. Of those playing regularly in the 1900 County Championship not one had a career which stretched back to 1875. In middle age Shrewsbury found that his muscles required more in the way of gentle exercise to build them up to match fitness, and his sessions in the indoor nets were perhaps more intensive than in his youth. The indoor shed at Trent Bridge had only been erected in 1898, but for many years prior to that Shrewsbury had practised in a shed near the Boat Inn at Beeston.

His achievements on the cricket field reflect this fanatical devotion to practice. The press were unanimous as to his position *vis-à-vis* his rivals. To quote the two leading reporters of the 1890s: 'Arthur Shrewsbury may without the least reservation be described as the greatest professional batsman of the day' and 'Arthur Shrewsbury stands out in bold relief among the cricketers of today as the professional batsman *par excellence.*' This first comment came from the pen of Charles Pardon, the editor of Wisden, the second from C. W. Alcock, editor of the rival Lillywhite Annual. Both writers use the word professional quite deliberately. Shrewsbury was not the first man to earn his living playing cricket, but the manner in which he dedicated himself to perfecting his craft must entitle him to be the first of the modern school of professional batsmen.

Arthur Shrewsbury was born on 11 April 1856 at the family home in Kyte Street, New Lenton. His paternal grandparents came from the adjacent village of Beeston, whilst his mother's family – the Wraggs – hailed from Ripley, a small town just over the border in Derbyshire. Arthur's parents married in 1843. William Shrewsbury was then only 19 and Mary Ann Wragg, his bride, 21. The couple set up home in Willoughby Street, New Lenton, William's mother, now a widow, having a small shop in Park Street, a few hundred yards away.

Lenton today is merely a suburb of Nottingham, passed through on the journey between the centre of the city and the university. A hundred and forty years ago however, Old Lenton consisted of a cluster of houses near the White Hart, and New Lenton, a quarter of a mile up the road, was two or three streets of new dwellings bordering on The Park, an expanse of green which ran up to the rocky outcrop of Nottingham Castle. To the south of Lenton water meadows stretched down to the river Trent. The railway line between Nottingham and Derby had recently been opened and alongside the line industrial development was soon to transform the countryside.

The young couple had their first child, Joseph, in 1843. He was followed by Mary Elizabeth (1846), Amelia (1848), Louisa (1849), Edward (1852) and William Junior (1854), so that Arthur's arrival in 1856 brought the total in the family, with parents, to nine. After Arthur came two girls, both christened Maria – neither survived into their second year.

Just prior to Arthur's birth the family had moved from Willoughby Street to nearby Kyte Street. When Arthur was eight the family moved again, to a terraced house in Wellington Square, which is in Nottingham itself, and Arthur, with his brother William, was sent to school at the People's College, only a short walk from their new home. At this time William Senior was employed as a draughtsman-designer in the lace firm of J. T. Hovey of Stoney Street, Nottingham.

All four Shrewsbury boys, Joseph, Edward, William and Arthur, took an interest in cricket, an interest which was inherited from their grandfather, Joseph Shrewsbury, who played for the Beeston team in the 1820s. The earliest known Beeston match occurs in 1792, but unfortunately the names of the players are not published and therefore it is not possible to discover whether a connection between the family and cricket goes back a further generation.

Arthur's father does not appear to have played cricket at any serious local level. At least his name does not feature in any published matches, though it must be admitted that few scorecards involving Lenton were printed in the press of the 1840s. The name of Wragg crops up occasionally and it is believed that Arthur's maternal uncles were fond of the game and that they played for Lenton – certainly there was a cricketer surnamed Wragg in the Lenton team of the 1840s.

The first newspaper mention of Arthur's cricketing bent comes in May 1867, when Arthur and brother William represented the People's College against High Pavement School. A second match in August also contains their names. Arthur was then 11 and William 13. In retrospect it is worthy of note that Arthur's classmate, the future England cricketer, Will Scotton, was not in the College team.

In the same year as these historic matches, the Shrewsbury

family moved house once again, to 51 Queen's Walk, Nottingham, and then two years later they finally moved to 2 Queen's Road, which being on the corner of two roads was also known as 2 Arkwright Street. The premises was in fact the new Queen's Hotel with William Shrewsbury senior as licensed victualler.

The Queen's Hotel, recently refurbished, stands today an isolated building in a sea of redevelopment. In 1869 it marked the beginning of The Meadows, an area of cheap terraced two-storey brick houses which spread down to Trent Bridge with Arkwright Street as the main thoroughfare, lined with small shops. Opposite the Queen's was and is the Midland Railway Station and much of the Queen's trade, indeed its *raison d'être*, would come from the people leaving the station for their homes in The Meadows or *vice versa*. It was an excellent position for a public house and Arthur's father, who must have been almost as ambitious as his famous son, saw the inn's potential. There were other places of refreshment in The Meadows, but the Queen's was a cut above them.

The young lads became members of a local cricket club, Meadow Imperial, and the batting averages for the Club in 1871 show 15-year-old Arthur at the top with 9 innings, 2 not outs, 28 not out as his highest and a total of 144 runs. William, well down the list, made 36 in 12 innings.

The principal local club in Nottingham during the 1860s and 1870s was Nottingham Commercial. With its home ground at Trent Bridge its eleven usually contained half-a-dozen county men and its fixtures were against major clubs in the Midlands rather than other Nottingham sides. Arthur's success with Meadow Imperial encouraged him to join the Commercial Club for the 1872 season. The report on the club's opening trial, at Trent Bridge on 6 May, noted: 'A. Shrewsbury, a new member, is the only player calling for special notice.' He made 16 not out.

A month or so later, Arthur appeared in his first important match on the County Ground, Lace v Hosiery. The title reflected the nature of Nottingham's staple industry and wealth. Arthur, having followed his father's occupation, was an apprentice draughtsman in the lace trade. This qualified him for the great annual contest between Lace and Hosiery. Six Notts county players took part in the 1872 match, but the cricket was dominated by the unknown sixteen-year-old, Arthur Shrewsbury, who scored 44 unbeaten in a total of 89.

As if to welcome this new recruit to the ranks of famous Notts batsmen, Trent Bridge Cricket Ground was being thoroughly modernised in 1872. The old single-storey, go as you please, pavilion, which was little more than an extension of the interestingly ramshackle Trent Bridge Inn, was at last abandoned in favour of a modern two-storey edifice with plate-glass front and two wings of covered seating. Not everyone agreed with the change as a letter to the press demonstrated: 'I deplore the building of a holy of holies in which the committee may sit, separating them from the common herd; the whole paid for from the sixpences of our cricket-loving townsmen.'

This holy of holies, however, was a clear indication of the importance of cricket in Nottingham and the importance of Nottingham in the world of cricket. William Clarke in the 1830s had established Nottinghamshire as a powerful cricketing county; he had laid out Trent Bridge. The metropolis had then beckoned him and for the final ten years of his life – he died in 1856 – his native town had rarely seen him. First he had been employed at Lord's and then he created the All England Eleven. This wandering side had for several years placed inter-county matches in the shade and not until 1859/60 did Nottinghamshire recover sufficiently to form a County Club run by an elected committee.

The immediate result of 'committee cricket', as George Parr, the Notts captain, termed it, was that county matches began to be played on a regular basis and because of this the Committee inaugurated, in 1861, the annual Easter match, played on Easter Monday and Tuesday, when twenty-two young hopefuls challenged the County First Eleven.

Both Arthur and brother William were busy cricketers in 1872. Arthur played not only with the Commercial and Lace Cricket Clubs, but also remained with Meadow Imperial and joined the Castle-Gate Club, which later developed into the well-known Notts Castle Club. Brother William was as ubiquitous as Arthur and cropped up as Privateer Shrewsbury in the Robin Hood Rifles team as well as organising his own eleven on The Meadows recreation ground.

It comes as no surprise to find that Arthur Shrewsbury applied for a place in the Notts Colts team for 1873 and was accepted. Although played on 14 and 15 April, the match was blessed with beautiful weather and some 6,000 spectators attended on the first day with another 4,000 on the second. Shrewsbury 'bats with carefulness and ease and is a most promising player' noted the correspondent for the *Nottingham Journal*. He was not too enamoured with all he saw however: 'The handsome new pavilion is almost entirely completed. It is a sightly structure and the interior is exceedingly well-appointed. We would suggest however that some suitable accommodation should be provided for those connected with the press.'

Shrewsbury made 35 of the 147 which the twenty-two colts totalled in their first innings. It was easily the highest score and he won the prize bat. Going in directly after Shrewsbury was Will Scotton, who had also performed well in local cricket in 1872. On 12 May Shrewsbury played at Lord's for the first time. He opened the batting for Fifteen Colts of England against MCC and was one of the three Notts representatives, the others being John Wheeler and William Shelton. Wheeler and Shelton had the misfortune to be the second and third victims of a hat-trick performed by the Notts bowler Alfred Shaw, who was a member of the MCC ground staff and at the time the most effective bowler in England. Shrewsbury made 4 before falling to the other great Notts and MCC bowler, George Wootton. In his second innings however Shrewsbury was 16 not out when the Colts won.

Arthur Haygarth, in his 'MCC Scores and Biographies', publishes under the scorecard of this match a brief biography of Shrewsbury. It was written in 1876, when Shrewsbury's career extended to only a dozen or so county matches: 'He is a most promising batsman, and, though but 20 years of age when this biographical notice was written, he had already highly distinguished himself, and nearly, if not quite, reached the top of the tree. His wrist play is elegant; he drives well; he possesses strong defence; and his style is shaped in the best school. His fielding is safe and excellent; he is a sure catch, with a quick return ... his future career will be watched with much interest by all true lovers of the noble science. Arthur is also a good football player.'

On Whit Monday, Shrewsbury opened the batting for the Next Fifteen of Notts against the First Eleven, scoring an excellent 25 and being partnered by George Royle, an amateur whose career in the lace trade prevented him from playing much county cricket. However, he remained a life-long friend of Arthur's and following his retirement from business served on the Notts Committee from 1894 to his death. He was also secretary of Lace CC. In a second match in August, Next Fifteen v First Eleven, Shrewsbury opened the batting with Will Scotton. Both were dismissed cheaply by Alfred Shaw, whose bowling was a major factor in Notts sharing the Championship title of 1873 with Gloucestershire, this being the first year when the rule banning players from representing two counties in the same season was enforced.

The most important feature of the local Nottingham season was the formation of the Meadow Willow Cricket Club. This club's appearance seems to coincide with the disappearance of Meadow Imperial as a cricket team, but three of the Shrewsbury brothers, William, Arthur and Edward, played in November 1873 for Meadow Imperial Football Club. From the few scattered newspaper reports Meadow Willow Cricket Club was apparently very much a part of the Shrewsbury family, with brother Joe as sometime secretary and the headquarters as the Queen's Hotel. William, Arthur and Joe appear regularly in the ranks of its eleven over the next few years, during which time it developed into one of the leading clubs in Nottingham. The team played on the Meadows recreation ground within walking distance of the Queen's.

Shrewsbury played for the Notts First Eleven against the Colts in the Easter Match of 1874, scored 2 and was seen no more during the summer in any matches published in the local press. The reason for his absence from the cricket field was rheumatic fever, which affects the joints, and to which teenagers can be prone in cold, damp conditions. Recovery back to complete fitness is sometimes a long process, as it appears to have been in Shrewsbury's case. The illness, which is non-infectious, tends to run in families and the fear of a recurrence was to influence Shrewsbury's way of life and attitude throughout his cricket career. The fear was not helped by his tendency to hypochondria.

His re-appearance on the cricket field occurred in the Colts match of 1875 – this time Easter fell very early, March 29, and Shrewsbury was dismissed without scoring. His brother, William, however, playing for the Colts, made 16 in their second innings and 'was much praised for his batting'. Arthur caught him off the bowling of Alfred Shaw.

Notts played Derbyshire at Whitsuntide and since four of the regular players were engaged in the North v South game at Lord's, the Notts Committee gave four youngsters the chance for first-class cricket. Three were making their first-class debut – Alfred Anthony, the wicketkeeper, and the two former pupils of the People's College, Arthur Shrewsbury and Will Scotton.

Scotton opened the innings and made 6 and 8. Shrewsbury, batting at number three, made 17 and 10. It proved to be Scotton's only first-class county match of 1875, though being on the staff at Lord's he appeared in a number of good class matches during the summer. Shrewsbury was retained by the Notts Committee and played in every one of the eleven Notts fixtures.

There were ten counties of first-class ranking in 1875, but the arrangement of matches between them was left entirely to individual secretaries, with the result that Nottinghamshire, Yorkshire and Surrey played ten first-class inter-county matches, Sussex, Gloucestershire, Kent and Lancashire played eight, Middlesex and Derbyshire six and Hampshire four.

The notion as to which counties were entitled to be styled first-class was left to the sporting press, as was the accolade of 'Champion County', which was loosely decided by which county lost least matches, but the strength of the opposition was taken into account, especially that of Hampshire, while Derbyshire was regarded as very much on the fringe.

With so few matches played the county clubs did not employ a groundstaff of players, though each county ground had one or two bowlers who were attached to local clubs. The division between professional and amateur players was quite marked, and this division was emphasised in the various counties. On one hand Gloucestershire fielded an entirely amateur eleven, on the other Yorkshire and Notts were overwhelmingly professional. Lancashire and Derbyshire tended to the professional, the metropolitan and southern counties to the amateur. Middlesex, Surrey, Kent and Sussex had difficulty in fielding their strongest teams as the amateurs were available only erratically, but under the influence of the Grace family Gloucestershire fielded a fairly constant eleven. The Gloucestershire amateurs came under much criticism because their expenses were usually more than the cost of employing professionals.

Nottinghamshire cricketers frowned on the hypocrisy of the amateurs, who were paid large 'expenses'. The team in 1875 was captained by Richard Daft. Aged 39, Daft had played for Notts for over 20 years; he had set the tone of the Notts eleven by turning professional as soon as he realised he could not afford to play as a genuine amateur. An elegant batsman, he was an automatic choice for any representative Players side, and though now past his best had been regarded as the equal of any batsman in England. The proprietor of the leading sports emporium in Nottingham, as well as the owner of a small local brewery, Daft was too easy-going to make a success in business. The previous year the manager of his sports shop had fled to New York with his girl friend, having swindled Daft out of several hundred pounds, and the business went steadily downhill with Daft taking no more than a passing interest in it. The young Shrewsbury no doubt saw the state of Daft's affairs and the possibility of a properly run sports outfitters.

Fred Wild and William Oscroft opened the Nottinghamshire innings. The former was a collier from Eastwood, the village later to become famous through the writings of D. H. Lawrence; Oscroft came from a great cricketing family which had dominated the village of Arnold for fifty years. Jack Selby, the middle order batsman, came from another well-known cricketing family, his father and grandfather having both been on the fringe of the Nottingham side. Initially he had made his name as a sprinter, being trained by the old prize fighter, Bendigo, who spent much of his time at Trent Bridge. The leading all-rounder was Martin McIntyre, born, like Wild, in Eastwood, but the son of an itinerant Irish potato picker. His fondness for the bottle prevented him from any consistency on the cricket field, but on his good days he was quite excellent. The principal bowlers were Alf Shaw and Fred Morley, the most effective pair in England in the late 1870s. Both were employed at Lord's. Morley was from Sutton-in-Ashfield, a fast left-arm bowler and terrible batsman; Shaw, originally a farmhand, came from Burton Joyce. Accuracy of line and length were his tenets and the batsman generally grew weary before Alfred, with fatal consequences. Two veterans on the point of retirement in 1875 were Sam Biddulph, the wicket-keeper, and Jemmy Shaw, another left-arm bowler from Sutton.

Those then were the established Notts players. The youngsters competing with Shrewsbury were Henry Reynolds of Ollerton and Billy Barnes of Sutton, both all-round men, William Clarke of Old Basford, John Mills, one of three brothers who played for Wollaton and the young wicket-keeper, Alfred Anthony of Arnold. Two amateurs played occasionally, Robert Tolley, captain of the Commercial Club, and William Williams, a solicitor.

The team photograph of the year shows the Augustan Daft in the centre, with, on extreme right and extreme left, the brothers William and Arthur Shrewsbury – William played in just one 1875 match, against MCC at Lord's. The two young clean-shaven brothers seem out of place among the hirsute crew.

The usual path for a young professional to follow was to

secure an engagement to a wealthy amateur cricket club. MCC was the obvious example, and Shaw, Biddulph, Morley and Wild all had positions at Lord's. The other Notts men were scattered round the country, save for Daft. The Shrewsburys, however, even at the outset of their careers never fitted the traditional role of professional cricketer. In the case of Arthur, his illness in 1874 might have decided him against a permanent professional post, and being trained as a draughtsman meant that he had a decent trade to augment his match fees from the county. William married at the age of 19 and in 1875 also had a young son, Arthur Junior, to support. Like his brother he was in the lace trade and seemed to believe that a career in lace was better than that of a professional cricketer. Both, it would seem, had inherited their father's independent spirit and the thought of being tied by contract to the beck and call of some parochial cricket club was not to their liking. A contract to Notts County Cricket Club meant only that a player would make himself available for county matches – in 1875 some 36 days cricket over the summer.

During the 1875 season Shrewsbury scored 313 runs for Notts at an average somewhat over 17 and a highest score of 41 against Gloucestershire. In his review of the summer, C. W. Alcock noted: 'Shrewsbury is a sound batsman as well as a safe field and, I am inclined to think, the best young professional batsman introduced (into the Notts team) for many years.' Lillywhite's Companion however is not as definite and favours another: 'Of the young players, Shrewsbury and Barnes have both shown promise of future batting powers, the latter having it in his power to become first-class. Shrewsbury wants practice against slow bowling, but has played pluckily at times.'

Two splendid innings in June 1876 proved Alcock right and so impressed the experts at Lord's that Shrewsbury was chosen for the fixture of the season, Gentlemen v Players. Shrewsbury chose the headquarters of cricket to make his first fifty in a first-class match: 59 for Notts v MCC. It proved to be the highest innings of the game – MCC were dismissed for 64 and 90 – and one reporter noted that during his

innings Shrewsbury allowed only three deliveries to pass his
bat: 'wonderful if true'.

Promoted to open the innings with Daft in the next Notts
game, v Yorkshire at Trent Bridge, the pair added a record 183
before being separated. Daft was out for 81, Shrewsbury stayed
three and a half hours for 118: 'he was heartily applauded
and the sum of £14 10s was subscribed and presented to
the lad (not yet 21 years of age) for his truly great innings.'

Though he did little in the historic Gentlemen v Players
match, he ended the summer with another long innings of
65, going in at number three and carrying his bat through
the Notts innings – a little slow perhaps, but made in capital
style. Away from county cricket, Shrewsbury played in some
matches for the old All England Eleven founded by William
Clarke. The former Notts captain George Parr managed the
team which was captained by Richard Daft and was in effect
an unofficial Notts side. William Shrewsbury also played in
this team, which presumably was still financially worthwhile,
though the wandering team run by the Graces – the United
South of England Eleven – obtained the cream of fixtures in
this exhibition-type cricket, the so-called amateurs, with W. G.
in the van, being handsomely paid for their appearances.

Illness again troubled Arthur. At the close of the second
day's play at the Oval in Thomas Humphrey's benefit match,
Arthur was 19 not out, but was taken ill overnight and
travelled straight back to Nottingham on the morning of the
third day. He recovered sufficiently to play for Notts six days
afterwards, so presumably this was not a recurrence of rheumatic fever.

Nottinghamshire had been acclaimed County Champions
in 1875, but with W. G. Grace in tremendous form all summer, Gloucestershire took the 1876 title, and Yorkshire
pushed Notts into third place. Notts' weakness was a reliable
wicketkeeper, Biddulph having retired. Happily the ebullient
Mordecai Sherwin was among the colts tried for the post in
1876. The critics were unanimous in their praise of Shrewsbury's batting. His record of 603 runs at 26 per innings
placed him in the leading twenty batsmen in England.

As the season closed, Selby and Alf Shaw set off for Australia with James Lillywhite's team. The Lillywhite Companion noted: 'The English Twelve who sailed from Southampton in September, for five months cricket in Australia, Tasmania and New Zealand, are a strong team of professionals, especially in bowling. Daft, Lockwood and Shrewsbury would have materially strengthened the batting, but, pleasant as is such a trip to the sunny south, it is not everyone who can manage to leave England.'

This tour, though Shrewsbury was not involved and it is not known whether he was invited, was to have a great effect on Shrewsbury's life because it created a great friendship between Alf Shaw and Jim Lillywhite. Shaw acted as assistant manager, or rather gradually moved into the job as the tour progressed. By the time Lillywhite was ready to undertake his second tour four years later, Shaw and Shrewsbury were both to take a major role in its organisation. In the meantime Shrewsbury, busy in the lace trade, followed the exploits of Lillywhite and his men from afar.

Selby and Alf Shaw returned safely from their tour. Notts in great fettle won their first two matches. In the first game Lancashire needed only 92 to win, but Morley and Shaw, bowling unchanged, dismissed them for 46. In the second match Shaw picked up 10 for 72 as Kent were defeated by 239 runs. On returning home from this game however Shaw was struck down with severe bronchitis and was unable to play again during the summer. The team seemed to go to pieces and in August suffered four successive defeats by an innings: 'the cricket all round was lamentably weak, the bowling harmless, the batting unreliable and the field loose and wanting in dash.' Shrewsbury, like his county, batted well for the first three months of the season, and apart from county cricket hit a century for the Players of the North and had a good innings for the Players v Gentlemen. In August he looked stale. In all he played in twenty-two first-class matches, as opposed to fifteen the previous year. He also appeared in a few matches for the All England Eleven.

2 Shrewsbury Leads a Strike

The season of 1878 turned cricket from a national game to an international one. The summer marked the first tour of a representative Australian side to England. During Lillywhite's visit to Australia in 1876–7, the Australians had proved themselves the equal of the tourists. Now it was their turn to come back to England and demonstrate that this improvement in their cricket was no aberration. The visitors played their first match at Trent Bridge on 20, 21 and 22 May: 'the interest of all cricketing England centred in Nottingham on those days.' The weather was unpleasant and so was the bowling of Shaw and Morley. The Australians were dismissed for 63 and 76; Nottinghamshire won by an innings and 14 runs. About 7,000 watched the first day's play and 10,000 the second. The tourists soon recovered their poise, beating a strong MCC team in a single day and then the Yorkshire side by 6 wickets. The crowds rolled in to see this brand new attraction and so did the money. The usual terms on which the Australians played their matches in England was that they took 80 per cent of the gate – so that, although billed as amateurs, the players received perhaps twice as much as the *bona fide* professionals in the county sides. The matter came to a head at the beginning of September.

The Surrey County Club, in view of the great success of the Australians, asked James Lillywhite to select a team of professionals to play against the tourists at the Oval on 2, 3 and 4 September. The match was intended to be a trial of strength similar to the two 'Test' matches played by Lillywhite's side against the Australians in 1876–7. Lillywhite duly picked his team and the great contest was advertised. In the *Sporting*

Life of 29 August, however, the following letter was published: 'Sir, – Having observed at the Oval that we are announced to play against the Australians there on Monday, Tuesday and Wednesday, September 2nd, 3rd and 4th, we wish, through your columns, to inform the public, so that they may not be misled, that we are not engaged at all in the match and do not intend to play. We also beg to inform the public that it is not the intention of any of the recognised Yorkshire players to take part in the match. If, Sir, any letters may be addressed to you on the subject of our terms of remuneration, we beg to inform the public that we only asked for what we paid the Australians in our benefit match in the Antipodes. Signed, W. Oscroft, J. Selby, F. Morley, A. Shrewsbury, A. Shaw, W. Barnes, H. Jupp, E. Pooley and W. Flowers.'

It should be noted that seven of the signatories are Notts men and both Shrewsbury and Shaw are prominent. The players had asked for £20 and been offered £10. The match went ahead with a moderate English side, but still attracted large crowds. There were many letters on the subject in the press and the 'shamateur' status of the Graces was again aired. The MCC came in for a lot of criticism, and when the premier club had the nerve to state that it had always adhered to the principle that amateurs only receive their expenses, the reply was that 'the statement is, to use a mild term, hardly consistent with facts'. Shrewsbury had very strong feelings on the subject and was also adamant that the MCC was responsible for the artificial division of cricketers into amateur and professional and that the club determined to maintain this division, though it served little useful purpose.

It was not only in the matter of amateur status that Shrewsbury clashed with authority in 1878. During the Notts v Surrey match at Trent Bridge in mid-July the following appeared in the press: 'What fun they have been having these cricketers to be sure! Arthur Shrewsbury is said to have stopped one minute longer than he ought at the practice net during the match between Surrey and Notts at Nottingham and down comes the energetic captain with his fist of iron. For gross insubordination some punishment is necessary, and in this case the fine is an apology. "Apologize, never!" is the reply of the rebellious professional and the whole cricket world is let into the secret of a petty squabble that can only have one end. Shrewsbury is left out of the Middlesex and Lancashire out-matches and there came floating on the breeze whispers of a general strike among the professional cricketers of Notts.'

It should be pointed out immediately that the 'energetic captain' is not Richard Daft, the leader of the Notts team, but Captain Henry Holden, Chief Constable of Nottinghamshire and Honorary Secretary of Nottinghamshire County Cricket Club. 'Hell Fire Jack', as he was known, was an autocrat who tried to deal with the Notts cricket professionals in the same way as no doubt he dealt with his minions in the police force. In Shrewsbury, a young whipper-snapper of 22, the bluster of the Captain met its match. The teetotal Shrewsbury, with a keen business brain, could not be treated in the same manner as the McIntyres and Jacksons of cricket, or even like the 'civil and obliging' Fred Morley. Shrewsbury, even so early in his career, realised that the public paid to watch him bat and he was entitled to the respect not only of the public, but also the Notts Committee. Shrewsbury was indeed suspended for two matches, after which Captain Holden made quite a point of showing that there was no ill-feeling by personally driving Shrewsbury to Trent Bridge for the next match – the reinstated cricketer duly hit a 'faultless and splendid' 60, the highest innings of the game against Yorkshire, which was won in two days with an innings to spare.

The rift between Captain Holden and the players, Shrewsbury in particular, was healed, but only temporarily. The Captain did not attend the club's Annual General Meeting through illness, which was presumably genuine rather than diplomatic, since diplomacy was not his strong point. The accounts presented at the AGM give some indication of the profits made by the Australian amateurs; receipts for the match were £404 10s 6d – only one county match had receipts above £100. The amount paid to the Australians was £238 14s 7d.

For most of 1878 the weather was wet and the batsmen suffered. It was Jack Selby's great year. He headed the first-class averages, even putting W. G. Grace in the shade, Selby being the only player to average above 30. Shrewsbury played in all the major representative matches and a total of 24 games in all, but never reached three figures. The Notts side with seven wins from fourteen matches had the best record among the counties, but Middlesex, who played only six games were undefeated and the reporters were unable to agree which county deserved the title.

If the weather in 1878 had been poor, in 1879 it was grim. A heavy fall of snow forced the abandonment of the second day of the Colts Match and the matches against Lancashire (2), Yorkshire, Middlesex, and Gloucestershire were all drawn through wet weather. Shrewsbury struggled on the heavy wickets and scored few runs until August. He was not selected for the Players against Gentlemen at either Lord's or the Oval and was omitted from several other representative games, Oscroft and Selby being preferred. Will Scotton, the same age as Shrewsbury, finally gained a regular place in the county side: 'An astonishing leap to the front has been made by Scotton, one of the steadiest left-hand bats we have seen for a long time and who is, moreover, a punishing hitter.' Unlike his old school friend, Scotton had taken a professional engagement at Lord's in 1874 and 1875, then at the Oval in 1876. In 1877 he became landlord of the Boat Inn at Beeston, a pub near the cricket ground used by the Gentlemen of Notts Cricket Club.

The last Notts match of 1879 was at Trent Bridge, commencing on 25 August. The team scored rapidly on the first day and by the end of the second had dismissed Kent twice and won by an innings. Perhaps the reason for the haste was that half the Notts team were due to board the SS *Sardinian* at Liverpool on 28 August bound for Canada and a twelve-match tour of North America. Captained by Richard Daft, the other Notts members were Shrewsbury, Shaw, Selby, Oscroft,

Barnes and Morley. Making up the twelve were five York-shiremen, Tom Emmett, 'Happy Jack' Ulyett, Ephraim Lock-wood, William Bates and George Pinder.

The tour was promoted by a Nottingham business man with interests in Philadelphia, the team selected by Richard Daft and managed by the Notts assistant secretary, Edwin Browne. Shrewsbury's first experience of an Atlantic crossing was not a pleasant one – the voyage revealed such 'an abject state of suffering in some few instances, that in common pity I am compelled to draw a veil over the whole picture', wrote one reporter.

All the matches, bar one, were played against odds, usually twenty-twos, and the scoring was therefore not high. Apart from 66 against Twenty-Two of Canada, Shrewsbury's scores were modest. Edwin Browne commented: 'Arthur Shrews-bury, long-headed and shrewd and a careful and elegant bat.'

It is more than probable that during the ten-week tour – the team landed back in Liverpool on 4 November – Shrews-bury and Shaw finalised their plans to open a business. In 1880 the new partnership launched 'The Midland Cricket, Lawn Tennis, Football and General Athletic Sports Depot' in rented premises at 85, Carrington Street Bridge, Nottingham. The shop was only a few hundred yards from the Queen's Hotel, which made it most convenient for Shrewsbury, but Shaw was living at the Prince of Wales Inn, Kilburn, London, and from April to the end of August was engaged by the MCC at Lord's. Apart from putting up half the capital therefore, Shaw's opportunities for an active role in the affairs of the new firm were very limited, a factor which much later was to cause ill-feeling between the partners. A description of the shop from a Trade Catalogue of 1889 states: 'The premises are four-storied in construction, of attractive design and ex-ceedingly commodious for conducting a large wholesale and retail trade. They comprise a handsomely appointed shop with plate-glass show windows, stock and showrooms, the whole being arranged in the most convenient manner.'

The 1880 English season was dominated by the coming of

the Second Australians. The tour opened in clouded circumstances. A definite announcement regarding the tour was not made until all the leading fixtures between the counties had been arranged and Lillywhite, who was acting as agent for the Australians, found it impossible to fix many county matches and had to resort to a mass of odds games against town eighteens. The cricket establishment did not view the visit with favour because of the continued amateur status of the players, despite the fact that the object of the tour was purely financial and that all the profits went directly to the players. The public, however, had the final say. The matches, even though they were little more than exhibition games, drew large crowds. The Australians offered to play 'England' with the proceeds donated to the 'Cricketers' Fund', but the MCC ignored the proposal. W. G. Grace tried to arrange a similar match at Lord's in July – again without success. In August, however, the counties, seeing an opportunity of making some money slipping through their fingers, began negotiations for matches in September. The Surrey Club raised the question of a match with 'England' once more and this time a firm date was agreed and Lord Harris invited to pick a representative England team. Shaw and Shrewsbury gathered together a North of England professional side to meet the Australians at Bradford in late September and the Notts executive arranged a county match with the Australians immediately following this Bradford game. This latter match being an extra county game, Captain Holden wrote to the Notts players saying that the terms agreed with the tourists were that they take half the receipts, and then, after expenses are paid, the remainder be divided between the eleven Notts cricketers. There can be little doubt that Shaw and Shrewsbury checked back at the receipts for the 1878 Australian match, and found that based on those figures the Australian players would be paid £19 each and the Notts players £6. It was little wonder therefore that Shaw, Shrewsbury and the other five leading Notts men told Captain Holden in no uncertain terms what he could do with his offer. Holden having spent money erecting temporary stands and putting out special advertising had little option but to agree under duress to the players' demands, which were £20 per man.

The match proved to be the most exciting ever played at Trent Bridge, Notts winning by one wicket due solely to Shrewsbury's batting. Notts began their second innings requiring 131 to win with a couple of overs left of the second evening's play. Daft sent in the tail-enders, Morley and Sherwin, and the score was 4 without loss at stumps. Boyle quickly dismissed both overnight batsmen on Saturday morning and with only 9 on the board, Shrewsbury came in to join Barnes. The wicket was terrible, but by the most careful tactics the two increased the score to 97, when Barnes was bowled by Moule. Oscroft helped Shrewsbury to take the total to 109 at which point an astonishing collapse occurred. Oscroft was bowled by Boyle, Selby went for a duck, Scotton failed to score, Daft made one and Flowers failed to score, taking the score to 120 for 8. Young William Gunn helped Shrewsbury to add nine, then the last man, Alf Shaw, supported Shrewsbury while the winning runs were made. Morley and Sherwin then rushed out of the pavilion and carried Shrewsbury shoulder high through an avenue of cheering spectators to the dressing room. The receipts for the match were 50 per cent up on the 1878 game. The Australians cleared £34 per man. The Notts players, if they had agreed to Holden's original proposal would have had £15 per man. But Holden paid the seven players who demanded £20 their full amount and then wrote to the press:

'Sir, – At a meeting of the Committee of the Notts County Cricket Club held this day (30 September), I was directed to forward the following correspondence for publication. I think it right to mention that it was decided to pay the four players who did not make the demand, £21 each. Signed, Hy Holden, Hon Sec, Notts CCC.' (The letters between Holden and the Shaw/Shrewsbury clique were then printed.)

So Holden paid the four other men an extra £1, but the club lost £160 staging the match. This was a considerable sum, which in fact virtually cancelled out the profits made from all the other county games in 1880. As can be imagined, Hell Fire Jack was now even less well disposed to Shaw and Shrewsbury than previously. Shrewsbury was the obvious trouble-maker, because Shaw had been a 'happy' member of the Notts side since 1864. The arrival of Shrewsbury heralded the discontent.

The Shaw and Shrewsbury match at Bradford against the Australians had proved a profitable undertaking. It was organised as the opening match of the brand new Horton Park Avenue Cricket Ground and the ground authorities were at once competing with Dewsbury and Huddersfield for first-class matches, given that Bramall Lane, Sheffield, was the centre for the majority of Yorkshire county games and the base for the County Club.

For 1881, with the Yorkshire executive allotting the home match with Notts to Bramall Lane, the Bradford authorities asked Shaw and Shrewsbury to bring a Notts team to Bradford to play the Yorkshire Eleven, in July.

As soon as Captain Holden got wind of the suggestion he took umbrage and wrote to Shaw and Shrewsbury on 9 February objecting to them arranging a county match, on the grounds that these could only be organised by the County Committees. Holden's memory however was rather short. Shaw replied reminding the Captain that Richard Daft had organised a Notts v Yorkshire game a few years previously without the Notts Committee raising an objection.

Shaw and Shrewsbury played for the Notts Eleven in the Eastertide Colts match and were invited to meet the Committee to discuss the question of the Bradford match. A further invitation was issued in the following week. Shaw and Shrewsbury refused to meet Captain Holden, but agreed to meet any three of the County Committee. As the committee declined, the position was a deadlock. Although the original irritant had been the Bradford match, in March Captain Holden had drawn up a new contract between the players and the club. Each of the principal players was invited to sign this contract, by which they agreed to make themselves available for all the county matches in 1881 and if selected they would be paid £5 for a loss or draw and £6 for a win. Shaw and

Shrewsbury, with five other players, Morley, Selby, Barnes,
Scotton and Flowers, objected to the contract on the grounds
that it bound the players to make themselves available for 36
days of the cricket season, but bound the Committee to nothing. The players might easily find themselves refusing other
offers of engagement on those 36 days and then discovering
that they had not been selected for the county. Shaw and
Shrewsbury therefore wrote back to Captain Holden saying
they would only sign such an agreement if the county guaranteed their places in the team for every county match. The
other five players were of the same mind.

The seven players then issued a three point ultimatum to
the Notts Committee:

1. That the match between Nottinghamshire and Yorkshire at
   Bradford should be allowed to take place under that title.
   (Shaw and Shrewsbury argued that if it was advertised under
   the title Shaw's XI v Emmett's XI, with the names of the full
   Notts and Yorkshire teams appended, the press and public would
   call it Notts v Yorks anyway, so Captain Holden was splitting
   hairs by objecting.)
2. That every player should be guaranteed a benefit after 10 years.
   (This clause was added because Captain Holden threatened the
   players that if they did not come to heel over the contract he
   would see none of them ever received a benefit.)
3. That the seven players should be engaged by the County Club
   for all County matches of 1881.

Although no agreement had been reached, all seven
players appeared in the first county match, against Sussex
at Trent Bridge on 26 and 27 May. The game was won by an
innings and Notts were under a new captain, William Oscroft,
Daft having announced his retirement at the age of 45. The
Committee went so far as to agree to engage five of the players
for all matches – Scotton and Flowers being excluded. The
seven however remained unrepentant and when Notts played
Lancashire on 2 June, the seven were dropped: 'the differences between the Committee and the players had not been
amicably settled.'

It looked now as if there would be a split in the Notts Committee. Shaw spoke to Captain Denison, who, although he had only rejoined the Committee in December 1880, had been vice-President of the Club in 1877 and MP for Nottingham for seven years. He verbally agreed that the Club would engage all seven players, if they apologised for not attending the Committee meeting in March. Captain Holden however refused to go along with Denison's compromise and the idea fell to the ground.

It was quite clear that the crux of the whole affair was the same personality clash which had led to Shrewsbury being suspended in 1878. On 19 July Captain Holden appealed to the MCC Secretary to mediate. Henry Perkins, Secretary at Lord's, actually got as far as persuading the seven players to take part in the next Notts match on 21 July against Surrey at the Oval. By that date the Bradford match had been played and, as forecast by Shaw, although called Shaw's XI v Emmett's XI in the fixtures, the press reporting the game called it Notts v Yorkshire. Spybey's Notts Cricket Annual covering 1881 notes: 'This match was arranged by T. Emmett on the part of Yorkshire and A. Shaw on that of Notts, and not by either County executive. It is virtually a contest between Notts and Yorkshire, and being so, it is given here as such, and is included in the season's averages.'

Captain Holden took note of the mediation of Henry Perkins, and then calmly proceeded to pick the Notts team for the Surrey match omitting Shrewsbury and Flowers. The seven players duly refused to take part and the impasse remained.

Curiously it was Flowers who finally broke the strike. He appeared in the match against Gloucestershire on 4 and 5 August at Clifton College – indeed he won that match by taking 12 for 85. Selby and Barnes returned for the next county game and they were followed by Scotton and Morley for the final two fixtures of the summer.

Shaw and Shrewsbury remained aloof throughout. When the cricket annuals covering 1881 appeared, the strike was dealt with in detail. The general argument was that the tremendous financial success of the Australians in 1878 repeated in 1880 made the English professionals 'who had previously comported themselves most becomingly' greedy for more money. Emotive phrases like playing for the honour of one's county (or country) rather than for purely financial gain, were used. In the present day context of cricketers going to South Africa or, a few years back, signing for Kerry Packer, the phrases have a very familiar ring to them. In the 1880s cricketers were by public acclaim on the same pedestal as pop singers and television personalities are today. In the era of Shaw and Shrewsbury, top cricketers were almost the only personalities who could regularly attract thousands, even ten thousand people, to pay to see them. The citizens who were asking Shaw and Shrewsbury to play for reduced fees were the extremely well-heeled gentlemen who ran the County Cricket Committees. The majority of the professional cricketers were ill-educated, easy-going men happy to please the Committees. Shrewsbury was, as the Notts assistant secretary had pointed out, long-headed and shrewd.

Shaw and Shrewsbury apologised to the Committee in the early summer of 1882 and were reinstated into the Notts side. The phrase 'to play in any match for which he might be selected on the usual terms' remained in the Notts' players' contracts. The bluff Captain Holden blundered on as the county secretary, but not for long. When the Australians played at Trent Bridge during their 1882 tour, the gallant captain 'forgot' to organise any lunch for them and when asked about it replied that amateurs found their own meals. The Captain went even further by telling the Australian captain that he, as Notts secretary, decided how long the wicket should be rolled between innings – it had nothing to do with either the team captains or the umpires. The next day some rude comments on Holden were discovered chalked on the door of the Australians' hotel in Nottingham. Holden openly accused the Australian manager of writing the remarks. It was later discovered that the comments had been the work of one of the hangers-on who followed the Australians.

In the middle of the summer, Holden tendered his resignation as Secretary and though the Committee asked him to stay in office until the Annual General Meeting, they were undoubtedly relieved to see him depart, or at least leave the most influential post in the Club – he remained as one of three trustees.

So far as can be discovered from Shrewsbury's papers, he was to remain on good terms with the Notts Committee from now until his death, though his partner Shaw was to end his county career on rather a sour note, but not of a financial nature.

3 The World Tour

In dealing with the aftermath of the 1881 strike, the story has run a little ahead of itself. James Lillywhite junior had made his debut in county cricket for his native Sussex in 1862. He had quickly developed into the leading left-arm medium-pace bowler in England and had been chosen to go to Australia with W. G. Grace's Team in 1873/4. In Australia he met John Conway, the fast bowler from Victoria, who was also a journalist. When Lillywhite decided to take a team out to Australia in 1876/7, Conway made all the arrangements in Australia; likewise when Conway managed the 1878 team to England, Lillywhite acted as agent in England. The 1876/7 tour to Australia was a very lucrative venture, Lillywhite actually paying the players double the money he had guaranteed them and making himself a good profit. Lillywhite was keen to make a second tour to Australia in 1878/9, but the Melbourne Club invited Lord Harris. With this tour having some rather unfortunate incidents, Lillywhite bided his time. In the summer of 1880 he wrote to Conway suggesting that a tour should take place in 1881/2.

The 1878 Australian team under Conway's management, after leaving England in September, had crossed the Atlantic and played several lucrative matches in America. Lillywhite decided to imitate the Australians, thus organising a round-the-world tour. The cost of such a tour would obviously be greater than the 1876/7 journey. Lillywhite therefore asked Shaw, who had helped in the management of the 1876/7 tour, to put up some of the money, and since Shaw was already in partnership with Shrewsbury it seemed sensible to include Shrewsbury, Shrewsbury being an automatic choice as a batsman for the tour. Also, if he helped to finance it, the number of players who needed a guaranteed fee was reduced to nine; Lillywhite, Shaw and Shrewsbury making up the twelve.

Therefore, while Shaw and Shrewsbury were involved in the strike against the Notts Committee in the spring and summer of 1881, they were also very busy making arrangements for the world tour. Most of the letters which Lillywhite wrote to Shaw and Shrewsbury, as well as those from Conway, and sundry other correspondence have been kept by the Shrewsbury family. It is therefore possible to reconstruct from the correspondence the difficulties and major points which arose during the planning stage, as well as the breakdown on the costs of such an undertaking, which was the first of its type by an English team.

John Conway in the autumn of 1880, on Lillywhite's instructions, began the task of negotiating with the various cricket authorities in Australia. He reported back to Lillywhite in November 1880 that the Melbourne Cricket Club would let their ground for 10 per cent of the gross receipts, except for the grandstand for which they required 35 per cent. He thought the terms pretty harsh and suggested that the East Melbourne Ground could be had at much better rates, maybe $7\frac{1}{2}$ per cent. In Sydney of course there was only the Association Ground (the home venue of New South Wales), so one had to accept whatever the Sydney people offered – probably 20 per cent. Conway enclosed his rough calculations:

MELBOURNE CRICKET GROUND
Probable attendance for a big match

Gate
1st day	10,000
2nd day	6,000
3rd day	10,000

26,000   at 1/- = £1,300 less 10 per cent = £1,170

Grandstand
1st day   1,500
2nd day   1,000
3rd day   1,800
                ─────
            4,300   at 1/- = £215 less 35 per cent = $\dfrac{134-10}{£1,304-10}$

The booths under the stand are all leased by the Club.
The expenditure nowadays would not be more than £300 with proper management.

SYDNEY CRICKET GROUND
Probable attendance for a big match

Gate
1st day   10,000
2nd day   6,000
3rd day   10,000
                ──────
            26,000   at 1/- = £1,300 less 20 per cent = £1,040

Grandstand at 2/-
1st day   1,200
2nd day   800
3rd day   1,200
                ─────
            3,400   at 2/- = £340 less 20 per cent = $\dfrac{272}{£1,312}$

The booths will realise at Sydney about £250 whereas £150 is my outside estimate for Melbourne. So that according to the above, the totals would be with booths

                Melbourne   £1,340
                Sydney   £1,512

'Of course this is a *fine weather* estimate and in our climate the chances are 50 to 1 on having fine genial weather throughout. Sydney expenses will be about the same as that of Melbourne.'

Conway continued: 'With anything like luck you must clear a thou' over each of your first matches in Sydney and Melbourne, and if the first two matches are interesting there is no knowing how successful the succeeding engagements may be. A grand combination match (i.e. Test Match) at

Melbourne and another at Sydney should draw well. The estimate I have made out for you represents a match played on Thursday, Friday and Saturday. There are times when it is judicious to play Friday, Saturday and Monday.

'Another thing you must bear in mind is that the expenses in travelling by steamer are now not quite half as much as they were formerly. By the splendid steamships of the Orient Company which do their passages quicker and more regularly, the P and O service, you could, for the team, get your passages for a mere song. So all things considered I think next cricket season here a very good time for the visit of an English Eleven.'

Conway's council was not confined to negotiations with Australian grounds and the cost of travel: 'If you bring a strong eleven with the best new blood and an eleven good enough to play Australia hard, there is a cartload of money waiting for you, but if you bring a weak lot you know as well as I do it won't go down. I would suggest to you about the following lot to bring, Bates, Lockwood, Morley, Shaw, Barnes, Shrewsbury, Pinder, Mycroft, Ulyett, Pilling, Selby and yourself (Lillywhite). That would be the finest possible combination of English talent and would draw thousands to witness their play.'

Some doubts surrounded the inclusion of the Yorkshire batsman, Ulyett, as he had caused some trouble during Lord Harris' 1878/9 tour, but he had topped the batting averages and Conway thought him absolutely essential. As he pointed out, the Victorians had quickly forgotten Midwinter's 'scurvy treatment' of the 1878 Australian team (Midwinter had abandoned the tourists very early on in order to play for Gloucestershire).

Shaw and Shrewsbury floated the idea of making all the players pay their own way and take a risk on the profits. Lillywhite, however, did not agree: 'I fancy it will be difficult to get the players to go out on a speculation and think that if we three find the coin and run the risk it will be best. It will take £300 each at least, perhaps £350 to make sure – say leaving out ourselves:

> 9 men at £50 each   £450
> passages to America and other expenses   £250

This will leave £200 out of the £900, which ought to be enough to meet every expense till we begin to play in America, unless some of the men wanted more than £50 before they started.'

The next financial discussion involved Conway's commission – they agreed after haggling to £100 plus 10 per cent of the profits in Australia, New Zealand and Tasmania, but nothing on the American profits, which they hoped would amount to £2,000, based on the information that San Francisco paid the 1878 Australians a guaranteed £400 for their match alone, which was a three-day affair against the local twenty-two.

Every time the England team goes to Australia the newspapers debate the minimum number required. This problem has remained unchanged since the days of Shaw and Shrewsbury. In 1881 it took so many weeks to travel to Australia that there was no chance of an injured man being replaced by a player shipped out from England. Lillywhite was in no doubt as to the number required: '12 will be enough, I can stand umpire and if any one gets hurt, bowl some of them out and hit a few fourers, but if wanted to look after things at any time, we can pick up plenty of umpires in Australia, old Sam Cosstick, Terry and many others, only it won't do to take a Melbourne man to Sydney. Lord Harris had enough of that.' (The reference was to the umpires being accused, wrongly, of being bribed on the 1878/9 tour.)

Having decided to go to Australia via America, it seemed logical to take in New Zealand before landing in Australia. Unfortunately this would mean playing matches in New Zealand in November, that country's wettest month. Lillywhite however drafted out a programme which involved arriving at Auckland on 24 November and leaving Invercargill on 16 December, thus arriving in Melbourne ready to play on Boxing Day. Lillywhite then sent to Shaw and Shrewsbury his ideas on the financial set up:

Expenses

12 men at £225 each	£2,700
Passages to America	250
Passages San Francisco to Auckland	600
Hotels in America, New Zealand and Australia for 22 weeks at £35 per week	770
Money for drink from Sept 4 to May 6 1882, 35 weeks at £18 per week	630
Passages from Australia to England via Orient Line	600
Conway's fee	100
Conway's expenses	100
extra expenses (say)	250
	£6,000

Receipts

Profits in America	£1,200
Profits in New Zealand	800
Three Matches in Sydney at £600 each	1,800
Three Matches in Melbourne at £600 each	1,800
1 Match at Brisbane (or 2 in Tasmania)	500
1 Match at Adelaide	500
8 Matches chosen from the following: Maitland, Newcastle, Bathurst, Goulbourne, Wagga Wagga, Albury, Beechworth, Sandhurst, Ballarat, Stawell, Warnambool, Hamilton, Castlemaine, Kadina at £200 each	1,600
	£8,200

When Conway learnt of the proposals he expressed the opinion that the players were being paid too much at £225 each. He also did not approve of playing in New Zealand in November, being of the opinion that January would be better and that the Australian fixtures could be split in two. Conway had opened negotiations with the various New Zealand Clubs but was insisting on a guaranteed lump sum for each match, rather than a percentage of the profits – he was trying to get £600 for five matches.

Out of the blue in early June an odd cabled message from England appeared in the *Melbourne Age*. It stated, 'A hitch has occurred in the ranks of the Professional Team. The Nottingham contingent threaten to pull out.' This threw Conway into a panic. If Lillywhite's team was not to include any Notts players, it would be a very weak one and command poor gates in Australia. Conway had emphasised to Lillywhite the need for the strongest possible team. On reflection Conway, not seeing any reports in the other Australian papers, assumed that it was an unfounded rumour and continued his discussions. In fact it was the garbled announcement that the seven Notts professionals had refused to sign their contracts with the Notts Club. Conway wrote to Lillywhite and eventually was told the facts.

Meanwhile in England Lillywhite, Shaw and Shrewsbury were tying up the loose ends: 'Do you think we can trust all the men, or would it be advisable to add a clause in the contract (in case of drunkeness, or behaviour, which would greatly injure the success of the undertaking), in which case we should have the power to inflict a heavy fine, say £20.' Shaw and Shrewsbury did not think this necessary. The debate on the final composition of the side was also discussed: 'Selby, I fancy, will be a better man than Flowers or Scotton for us, and we shall want the best batting we can muster.'

Conway was anxious to obtain the full details of the proposed side and again pressed the point about its quality: 'Now I want to impress upon Shaw, Shrewsbury and yourself,' he wrote to Lillywhite, 'that you must get the strongest team among the pros that England can produce and bring plenty of batting for that is what is required on our hard fast turf. The spec in a great measure depends upon the team. With Shaw, Morley and Mycroft and the other changes, viz Barlow, Bates and others, you do not require to weaken your batting by the inclusion of Peate (the Yorkshire bowler) who is I understand not strong with the bat. The following would be a grand team: Shaw, Morley, Mycroft (bring him with you), Barnes, Bates, Selby, Shrewsbury, Barlow, Gunn, Lockwood (or Hall) and yourself and Pilling. I do not think Charlwood good enough, but Tom Emmett is a rare good man if you are stuck.' (Conway had forgotten Ulyett.) Conway also sent a detailed programme and Lillywhite dropped a line to Shaw: 'Altogether the Australian arrangements seem to me very satisfactory, much more so than on the last occasion, as the idea of poor Freddy Grace (W. G.'s brother, who had died in 1880) taking out a team had got root there, which got us as you know into lots of trouble about grounds. This time we are alone and nothing of that sort will take place. By what I hear privately we shall go down there immensely with the best team we can take, as they are madder than ever on cricket.'

Lillywhite began bargaining with the various shipping companies. For the journey across the Atlantic, the Anchor Line charged 12 guineas sailing from London, the Cunard 15 guineas sailing from Liverpool. The latter made a faster crossing, which would enable the team to play an extra match in America. Cunard might also give some railway concessions. It was decided to travel on the Cunard Line, but pick up the boat at Queenstown in Ireland, because Shrewsbury had arranged two matches in England before the team left, against a Notts Castle XVI and at Holbeck, Leeds. Sailing from Queenstown allowed an extra day for these matches. The three promoters were determined to make every penny possible and a day spent travelling was a wasted day.

News reached England that a new ground was to be opened in Christchurch, New Zealand. On the previous trip the English team had discovered too late that the old Christchurch ground was open to the public. The Australian side had gone to the lengths of trying to get a bill through the New Zealand parliament closing the ground for their match, but the bill failed by one vote. Conway and Lillywhite had earlier discussed the possibility of putting another bill to parliament. Lillywhite noted: 'I hope Conway knows all about the new ground, all must pay and they expect us to open it, that alone will pay to go to N. Z., if we can get a good fair share of the gate, we can also force them to pay in Dunedin, so N.Z. looks rosy.'

This good news was balanced against various letters from America, of which the one below was typical:

From: *Staten Island Cricket and Base Ball Club*
New York August 22nd, 1881

Dear Sir,

Yours of the 13th ultim duly recd. Our club has been considering the matter of a match with your team, which we are anxious to arrange, but after trying the matter in every light we really find that we shall be unable. In a financial point of view we do not think that it would be at all satisfactory to your eleven, as cricket does not draw a good attendance in New York and, outside of the gate money, our club could not guarantee anything. In our match with Daft's XI (1879), where they had half the gross gate receipts the amount they obtained was comparatively small and our club was out some 300 to 400 dollars expenses, over and above their half of the gate receipts. But apart from this view of the case, our committee have not the time to give to making the match a satisfactory one.

It is a pity to have to say this, but it is unfortunately true. Our season has been a very quiet one and our men all being engaged in business are at that season of the fall very much tied down, and as they would not undertake a match without putting it through in first class style and not feeling able to give the necessary time for it, we are sorry to have to forego the pleasure it would have given us to play your team.

Yours truly
E. H. Outerbridge, *Secretary.*

So the profits in America, originally estimated at £2,000 and then £1,200, were dwindling.

Even in late August, with the side due to sail on 17 September, there were still problems with the final composition of the team. 'You will see, Mr M. P. Lucas answered promptly, I am sorry to say he can't go,' Lillywhite wrote to Shrewsbury, 'Flowers would be a good man, but I don't think he will go by what he said yesterday. What about Mr Docker from Derbyshire, he is a pretty good man, or do you think Gunn good enough? I suppose we must soon see about fixing on one. Emmett would go no doubt, or Scotton, Charlwood or Briggs.' Lillywhite ended with a reference to his own benefit and a match arranged between Shaw's XI and Lord

Sheffield's XI at Sheffield Park: 'A card of my match will be down shortly. £185–10 yesterday at Chichester. I spoke like *Gladstone*. What sort of fun at Earl Sheffield's.'

Having dealt with the arrangements for crossing the Atlantic, the next step was to check the Pacific crossings. The main money in the States was to be made in Philadelphia: was it possible to arrange some matches on the route between Philadelphia and San Francisco? 'It won't do to say we will play and then not be able, they would be down on us like 1,000 bricks. Shall I ask 1,250 dollars (about £250) for three days at Frisco or 1,500 dollars and let the others alone till we arrive and see what happens?' Lillywhite asked Shrewsbury.

The nine finally decided upon to make up the team were: G. Ulyett, W. Bates, T. Emmett, E. Peate (all Yorkshire), R. Pilling and R. G. Barlow (both Lancashire), W. H. Scotton and J. Selby (both Notts) and W. Midwinter of Gloucestershire. A lot of Conway's advice seems to have been ignored, with the absence of Mycroft and the inclusion of Peate.

On 15, 16 and 17 September the match against Sixteen of the Notts Castle Club was played. Peate performed the feat of four wickets in four balls and four good wickets at that – William Gunn, C. Wragg, Walter Marshall and Arthur Shrewsbury's brother William.

The serious feature of the game was the absence through illness of Arthur Shrewsbury. The team was given a great send-off at Nottingham station directly the match with the Castle Club ended, but Shrewsbury, suffering again from bronchitis, was forced to remain at home. There was some doubt about his participating in the tour at all, but Shrewsbury's doctor thought that wintering in the warm climate of Australia would be beneficial to his health, and at the end of September, Shrewsbury sailed direct for Australia via Suez.

In Philadelphia about 8,000 spectators turned up to watch the English team on the first day of their match there, but Philadelphia lost by an innings and the other four matches of the tour were financial failures. In San Francisco the only person in the sparse crowd who knew much about cricket demanded his money back! The total receipts scarcely covered

the expenses for the five matches as a whole. The team therefore arrived at the shipping offices in San Francisco with no
money to pay the £600 required for passage to Australia. At
this stage they had hoped to be £1,200 in pocket. Shaw
offered a cheque drawn on the Nottingham Bank, but only
after much argument was it accepted and the cricketers sailed
for Sydney. The SS *Australia* made the crossing to Auckland
in a record twenty days and reached Sydney four days later,
where the party were met by John Conway and Arthur
Shrewsbury.

Five up-country matches opened the tour, before the team
returned to Sydney for the first major fixture on 9 December.
To the great relief of the promoters, 7,000 turned up on the
first day and 20,000 on the second. In addition the tourists
won the game by 68 runs. With just a one-day match at
Cootamundra, the team went to Melbourne for the game with
Victoria. The batting collapsed and they were forced to follow
on 105 runs in arrears; four wickets went down for 73, at
which point Shrewsbury came in and played a 'rattling good
innings of 80 on a difficult wicket' carrying out his bat. The
steamer for Adelaide was persuaded to wait until the game
was ended, rain having interrupted play, and Peate's bowling
produced a win by 18 runs. Christmas was spent in South
Australia, after which the side returned to Melbourne to meet
Australia over the New Year. A high-scoring match spread
over four days was drawn, Ulyett, Selby and Bates being the
principal run-getters on the English side. About 40,000 spectators turned out – a quarter more than estimated – so at last
the money was rolling in. On the night the match ended the
team sailed for Dunedin and the first match of their New
Zealand leg. Three matches were played before the most important game at Christchurch. Great crowds had come into
the town for the match, but before play could begin the rain
set in and continued for four days. As previously noted this
was the first important match to be played on the Lancaster
Park Ground; by again persuading a steamship company to
delay sailing, a two-day match over Monday and Tuesday
was played, but the wickets were sodden and the opposition

feeble. All in all the visit to New Zealand was financially scarcely worthwhile, and the team returned to Australia for a final eight matches, including three against Australia and one against Victoria. In the first game, Shaw foolishly decided to bat on a damp, ill-prepared wicket and this cost the tourists the match. A weak Victorian team was beaten by eight wickets. At Sydney rain again affected the match which was lost and rain caused the final eleven-a-side fixture against Australia to be drawn.

Although he had a highest score of only 82, Shrewsbury averaged 38 in 12 first-class innings. In the batting table he came second to Ulyett, but the Yorkshiremen's average was boosted by an innings of 149.

Despite the financial problems in America, the games in Melbourne and Sydney proved popular and each of the three promoters went home with £700.

4 Profits and Records

The immediate effect of the 1881–2 tour so far as Arthur Shrewsbury was concerned was the improvement in his health, brought about by the avoidance of the English winter as much as the sunshine of Australia. He celebrated his 26th birthday whilst on board the SS *Chimborazo* and sometime during the tour or on the voyage home must have discussed with Alfred Shaw the question of putting some of the profits into the cricket outfitting business. The result was the opening of a factory under the title of the Gresham Works situated in Waterway Street, Nottingham. The street was bisected by Arkwright Street and like the shop in Carrington Street, the new factory was only a five-minute walk from the Queen's Hotel. Alfred Shaw, about the same time, left his public house in London and moved into the Belvoir Inn off Arkwright Street, but he was to remain there only about a year before he took his engagement in Sussex with Lord Sheffield. For twelve months or so therefore the two partners both lived within easy distance of their shop and factory and it would appear that the business rapidly expanded. In theory their chief rival was Richard Daft, whose sports emporium was at 1 Lister Gate, Lister Gate being at that time a continuation of Carrington Street. As has been noted earlier, however, Daft was no business man and certainly no match for the young ambitious Shrewsbury.

Shrewsbury's character contained some curious contradictions. According to several of his contemporaries, he was a shy, retiring man, always keen to return home directly a cricket match had ended. He did not mix easily with his fellow professionals. He was acutely sensitive about his baldness and

was never seen without a hat, or cricket cap. If at all possible
he would travel back to Nottingham each night from a
match, rather than spend the night away from home.

Yet at the age of 22 he was standing up to the bellicose
Captain Holden, a gentleman patently used to being obeyed.
Less than three years later Shrewsbury was the instigator and
ringleader of the strike against the authority of the Notts
Committee, even though he was the youngest of the cricket-
ers involved. With no business training he launched with
Shaw this cricket outfitters and ran it almost single-handed,
building it into one of the largest firms of its type in England.

Having made up the quarrel with the Notts Committee,
Shrewsbury was selected to play in the opening match of
1882 against Yorkshire at Trent Bridge, but was unable to
do so, and it was not until the match against the Australians
on 8 June that he finally re-appeared in the County side. In
a low-scoring, rain-affected game he hit an excellent 30. Despite the weather, the Australians proved as popular as on
their two previous visits to Nottingham, with about 25,000
attending the match.

Unlike previous seasons, however, Shrewsbury's batting
was very uneven. Against Surrey in the August Bank Holiday
fixture he compiled his first double century – 207 out of the
Notts total of 501. It was the highest score of 1882, and with
William Barnes he created a new first-class second wicket
record of 289 made in 270 minutes. In all Shrewsbury was
at the wicket 395 minutes and hit one five and 24 fours. It
was the highest individual innings ever made for Nottinghamshire and he gave only one chance. That magnificent score
accounted for virtually half Shrewsbury's aggregate for Notts
in 1882, though he played 15 other innings. His only other
really notable score was an unbeaten 43 for the Players
against the Gentlemen at Lord's. In local cricket he created
another record by hitting 188 not out for Meadow Willow
against Forest Wanderers. Meadow Willow made 291 for 3.
(In another report Shrewsbury's score was 170 not out.)

Nottinghamshire won the Championship title jointly with
Lancashire in 1882. Barnes headed the county batting table,

but most credit for the success went to the bowling firm of Shaw and Morley – Morley refused to play in Notts' final game of the season because he was about to depart for Australia with Ivo Bligh's Team 'to bring back the Ashes'. It was a sad departure for Fred Morley, because on the voyage out he was seriously injured when the ship was in collision, and later he died due partly to the injury he received – he played in just one more Notts match.

Although Arthur Shrewsbury still lived at the Queen's Hotel, there had been a number of alterations in the circumstances of his immediate family since his father had moved in thirteen years earlier. Elder brother Joe had married and was living in Walter Street, near the Arboretum; Mary Elizabeth had married a Mr Radford and had two sons, Albert and Joseph; Amelia had married a Frenchman, Eugene Edward Vasseur, but was by 1881 a widow with two daughters and had returned to the Queen's as manageress. Arthur's youngest sister Louisa still lived at home and worked as a waitress at the Queen's. Of his other two brothers, William Junior had married Emma Walker at the age of 19 and by 1883 had had six children, two of whom had died in infancy; Edward had also left the family nest but still lived in Nottingham. Joe and William were in the lace trade and about 1883 they formed a partnership with Arthur – Shrewsbury Bros – and leased a number of lace machines situated in the Player's Factory in Radford Road, Nottingham.

The 1882 season had been financially a particularly good summer for the County Club. The profit on that year alone amounted to over £600 and to this could be added the £300 surplus from the previous balance. Captain Holden, who was not the man to act as Secretary, had therefore made a great success of his other office as Treasurer and won a great deal of praise when he formally resigned at the Annual General Meeting in January 1883. The other resignation at this time was of the captain, William Oscroft. He had made his debut in the same season as Alfred Shaw and had been an immediate success, but of recent years his batting form had become very erratic. In September 1882 illness which was diagnosed as locomotor ataxia, the main symptoms of which were giddiness and an inability to control the muscles of his arms and legs, forced him to give up cricket entirely. The Notts Committee chose Alfred Shaw as the new captain for 1883 and Henry Bromley as the new Honorary Secretary and Treasurer. The main criticism at the AGM was that the Committee, with a large balance in hand, did not increase the number of county matches so as to give some of the younger players more opportunity. In retrospect this criticism was quite justified, for by the end of the 1880s Notts found themselves losing ground to Surrey and Lancashire, both of which counties increased their fixture list to include several minor counties, while at the same time employing a few youngsters as a ground-staff. It was fifteen years before Notts acted in this direction, by which time the county had fallen to the bottom of the County Championship, or thereabouts.

In the meantime the summer of 1883 commenced with the Whitsuntide match with Surrey and an overwhelming victory for Notts. The southern county were dismissed for 87 and 43 with Notts' new captain taking 7 for 22 in the second innings. From the batting viewpoint the match provided a new pair of openers – Arthur Shrewsbury and Will Scotton. The old school friends added 40 before Scotton was caught and bowled by Roller for 22. Although Shrewsbury remained as an opener for the rest of the season, Scotton gave way to one or other of the amateurs, Charles Wright or Johnny Dixon. Wright was in his second year at Cambridge, hit an excellent hundred in the University match and directly afterwards was drafted into the Notts side, playing in nine games, but with a total lack of success. Dixon, a prolific batsman in Notts club cricket and an excellent soccer player, later capped for England, played four times for Notts in 1883, but, due to nerves, did little. The great young prospect was in fact neither of these amateurs but William Gunn. In 1882 Oscroft had regarded him as the best up-and-coming player in the county and when Notts had played the Australians and the Committee had chosen Fred Butler instead of Gunn, Oscroft, although captain, had stood down to allow Gunn to play.

Oscroft was later to say: 'A finer cricketer never walked in
two shoes. I would rather watch Gunn make 50 than W.G.
or Shrewsbury 100'. Gunn's career was to follow that of
Shrewsbury, and in founding the sports firm of Gunn and
Moore, Gunn was to emulate Shrewsbury in his business as
well as his cricket.

Unlike the previous year, Shrewsbury had no one great
innings to boost his average. His highest score came against
Sussex at Trent Bridge. Sussex were dismissed for 61, Alfred
Shaw returning the remarkable analysis of 40–26–20–4 and
Arthur then reached 96 not out by the close of the first day.
He 'was unfortunately run out after adding just two to his
overnight total. His other large innings for Notts was quite
similar. On August Bank Holiday Monday, Notts, having dismissed Surrey for 236, were 73 for 1 at the close with Arthur
36 not out. He was caught out the next day on 97. It was
during this match that a colt, John Pearson of the Worksop
Club, was brought into the side in emergency as a batsman,
was put on to bowl fifth change and took three wickets for
one run in 13 balls. The performance was a complete fluke,
for he rarely bowled even in club cricket.

Outside county matches, Shrewsbury played in most of the
other representative games, including Gentlemen v Players at
Lord's, when he scored 40 and 48. The match was notable
for a piece of fielding. The *Daily News* reported: 'The ball was
hit very hard (by A. G. Steel) and Shrewsbury dashed in,
falling forwards and reaching it about a foot from the ground;
although he fell and grazed his arm along the grass, the Notts
man held the ball, and thus brought off one of the cleverest
catches ever witnessed in London.'

On the dry, fast wickets of 1883, Shrewsbury reached
1,000 runs for the first time in his career. He came second to
Barnes in the Notts averages and well in the top twenty for
the country as a whole. The Notts batting overall was strong,
but the bowling was lacking poor Fred Morley, his place being
taken by Walter Wright, a left-arm medium-pace bowler from
Hucknall. He proved quite effective for a few seasons until he
fell out with the Notts Committee over terms and went to

play for Kent. This bowling weakness meant that though Notts lost only one match, they won only four, the other seven being drawn. More and more attention was being paid in the press to the county results set out as a league table, with least matches lost as the criterion for supremacy. Notts played 12, won 4, lost 1, whilst Yorkshire played 16, won 9, lost 2. There was a reluctant consensus of opinion among cricket reporters to award Notts the title of County Champions, but the business was rather unsatisfactory.

In the spring of 1884, the name of the cricket outfitters was altered from the vast 'Midland Cricket, Lawn Tennis, Football and General Athletic Sports Depot' to 'Shaw and Shrewsbury', which must have been a relief to correspondents. Their famous trade mark of a kangaroo and emu with a cricket bat between them was introduced about 1886.

Notts progress in 1884 was one of continuous success, a success materially assisted by the establishment of a regular pair of opening batsmen in Shrewsbury and Scotton. Their best partnership was 119 against Sussex at Hove; this was then dwarfed by Shrewsbury and Gunn who added 266 for the fifth wicket, which created a new world first-class record for that wicket, beating 261 made by W. G. Grace and W. O. Moberly at Cheltenham in 1876. The record which Shrewsbury and Barnes had created in 1882 for the second wicket had only lasted a single season; this new one survived eleven years. It probably was the origin of the old cricketing story of the Notts captain winning the toss at Hove and Shrewsbury and Gunn batting whilst the rest of the team went down to the beach for the day, though in reality Notts batted second and their innings was spread over two days.

Shrewsbury batted six and a half hours and was run out on 209, a new personal, as well as Notts, individual record. The season saw another visit from the Australians. Shrewsbury appeared in all three Tests, his best cricket being at Old Trafford where he made 43 out of a total of 95 all out.

Notts ended the year with nine wins out of ten matches, the other game being a moral victory, and there was no doubt that the county deserved the championship title. Dick Attewell, the medium-pace bowler from Keyworth, who had been given a thorough trial during the 1881 strike, proved most effective and partnered Shaw in preference to Walter Wright.

The arguments regarding payment returned with the Australians. Shrewsbury, Barnes and Flowers refused to represent the Players of England against the tourists for the £10 per man offered by the Yorkshire Committee – the match was being staged at Bramall Lane. The match went ahead without the trio and was easily won by the Australians – the attendance was over 60,000. The press generally gave the Notts players unfavourable reports: 'Cricket is not a source of personal benefit to those who guide the destinies of the leading clubs, and it is altogether unlike business where capital is mostly dependent on paid skill and labour ... every well-wisher of the sport will regret the attitude they have thought fit to take.'

Shrewsbury was obviously of a different opinion.

Whilst Shaw and Shrewsbury were busy helping Notts to win the title, they were also occupied, in partnership with Jim Lillywhite, arranging the second of their tours to Australia. This time they were not making the error of touring America and New Zealand, but confining themselves to Australia.

John Conway was again charged with the task of arranging the matches for the tour and again impressing on the trio the importance of a strong team. This task was more difficult than might be expected. The two Surrey amateurs, W. W. Reid and E. J. Diver, declined an invitation. The best wicket-keeper of the day, Pilling of Lancashire, was on medical advice forced to decline, as did Mordecai Sherwin, the Notts wicketkeeper, though his reason was probably his football commitments. The Lancashire batsman, Barlow, and Walter Wright of Notts both refused. The composition of the party which sailed from Plymouth on 19 September was: W. Barnes, W. Attewell, W. H. Scotton and W. Flowers of Notts; G. Ulyett, W. Bates, R. Peel, J. Hunter of Yorkshire, J. M. Read of Surrey and J. Briggs of Lancashire, plus the three promoters. According to Jim Lillywhite, he was the manager and

Alfred Shaw the captain, but Shaw's version was that Lilly-white was umpire, Shaw manager and Shrewsbury the captain. The latter situation was nearer reality. Shaw commented: 'The team was not only a splendid one in the cricketing sense, but it was a happy and well-conducted family in a social sense. Experience had tamed the wild spirits of one or two members of the party, who had visited the Land of the Golden Fleece and of bountiful hospitality on previous occasions.'

The team opened its programme in Adelaide, playing two matches, the attendance at both being sparse. The first important game was then staged at Melbourne against the colony. Members of the 1884 Australian side to England refused to play, probably due to the Notts players refusing to play against them in Sheffield. Shrewsbury's innings of 80 was the highest of the match, which gave the visitors an easy win. Moving on to Sydney for the match against New South Wales, again the 1884 Australians declined to play, but about 30,000 attended over the three days, which pleased the promoters.

The first match against the 1884 Australians was promoted by the South Australians at Adelaide, each team being guaranteed £450. Murdoch, the Australian captain, objected to Lillywhite standing as umpire, so a local man stood and gave some very strange decisions, mostly against Murdoch's men, but they could hardly complain. The English side won by eight wickets and the South Australians lost money.

Ill-feeling between the 1884 Australians and the tourists continued and the former all refused to play in the New Year holiday match for Combined Australia at Melbourne. The Victorian Cricket Association retaliated by banning Murdoch and his men from any match under the Association's jurisdiction. The English side beat the weak Australian team by 10 wickets. One of the most unexpected matches was at Candelo, which town, with a population of only 200, had raised the £300 guarantee to stage the game. Virtually everyone within a fifteen-mile radius turned up – about 150 buggies and 600 on horse-back, despite an admission charge of 2/6d.

Another remarkable country match was played at Moss Vale, where the tourists batted from noon on the Wednesday to 4 o'clock on Thursday, hitting 432, and then bowled out the whole of the twenty-two for 14, with Peel taking 18 wickets for 7 runs. After six successive odds matches, the team returned to Sydney for a game against New South Wales the second day being 26 January – a public holiday celebrating the founding of the colony. The 1884 Australians still refused to play. Showers made the first day quite miserable, but about 7,000 spectators were present. On the second day, being the holiday, 10,000 paid, but after seeing New South Wales dismissed for 60 – Peel taking 7 for 27, the rain returned in earnest and flooded the ground. Only about 1,000 came on the last day, when the tourists won by an innings, and the weather continued to be so miserable that everyone was glad that the English side did not need to bat a second time.

Three matches were played in Queensland. At Brisbane only 5,000 watched on the Monday in spite of it being proclaimed a holiday. In the rich gold mining town of Gympie, Scotton won 250 gold shares for making the highest score.

The return match against Combined Australia began at Sydney on 20 February. A. Bannerman and Bonnor (of the 1884 Australians) 'having probably seen their folly' accepted invitations to play, and with Spofforth also available (he had had to stand down previously through injury), the Australians were for the first time well represented. The quarrel between the 1884 Australians and the English team had been made worse because of the animosity between John Conway, the agent for the tourists, and Murdoch. In January, Lillywhite had dispensed with Conway and replaced him by C. W. Beal of New South Wales, who had managed the 1882 Australians in England. This action no doubt helped to improve relationships. The match at Sydney proved to be one of the most exciting, with the Australians winning by 6 runs. The result would have been different but for the action, or inaction of Barnes, who refused to bowl in either innings, though asked to do so by Shrewsbury, the captain. The reason for

Barnes' refusal is not known, but it certainly swung the game
Australia's way, since the wicket was particularly suited to
Barnes' deliveries. The row between Shrewsbury and Barnes
was not of long duration, but it brought into focus the difference between Shrewsbury and the rest of the players,
although all were professionals. Like Shrewsbury, Barnes was
at loggerheads with the Notts Committee on several occasions
during his twenty-year career. In Shrewsbury's case it was a
matter of principle and finance, in Barnes', it was unruly
behaviour brought about by too much drink, and eventually
this resulted in his being permanently dropped from the
county team.

There were two more important matches on the tour, both
against a Combined Australian Eleven. The first in Sydney
ended in an eight-wicket victory by Australia. The first two
days were fine, with big crowds and the teams evenly
matched, but rain on the second evening produced a difficult
wicket and the English team collapsed against Spofforth and
Palmer.

In the final game in Melbourne, Australia batted first but
were dismissed for 163. The tourists quickly built a first innings lead and Shrewsbury scored his only hundred of the
season, 105 not out. Australia tumbled to an innings defeat
and the result was so obvious from the second morning that
the attendance after the first day was poor. The Melbourne
Club generously gave the visitors all the receipts from both
ground and grandstand.

The leading Australian critic, Felix, gave this account of
Shrewsbury's innings: 'His play throughout was a treat to
look at, and that neat and effective stroke of his between
square-leg and mid-on is worth copying. He made a large
number of his 105 in this spot. His defence was splendid, his
cutting clean and telling, his timing could not well be ex-
celled, and his care and judgment in dealing with enticing
balls to the off formed a lesson which young cricketers, and
indeed some old ones, could study with profit. During his long
stay at the wickets, Shrewsbury never once lost his patience
and on returning to the pavilion after his masterly and fin-

ished exhibition of batting, he was greeted with loud and long continued applause.'

A final odds match in Adelaide closed the tour. Jim Lilly-white ended his review of the visit with: 'It is rumoured that some of Murdoch's men (i.e. 1884 Australians) will be included in the Australian team visiting this country in 1886. I hope they will not be, but if they are, I trust the players of England will meet them on every occasion in which they are chosen, and make the trip as pleasant and profitable as possible for them, thus returning good for evil.'

The team, apart from Shaw, who had left several weeks before to start his engagement with Lord Sheffield, left Australia aboard the SS *Potose* on 4 April. Half the side left the ship at Naples and travelled overland, but Shrewsbury remained aboard until docking at Plymouth, and did not reach Nottingham until 16 May, too late to appear in the opening Notts match of the 1885 season. Although the profits from the tour were not as high as they might have been had Murdoch and his friends not boycotted many of the matches, the promoters made £150 each on their layout of £450.

5 England's Best Batsman

Shrewsbury returned home to the Queen's, but 1885 saw several changes of the inhabitants there. His father, now 60 and a relatively wealthy man, decided to retire, and moved to a place in the country – Ebenezer House at Fiskerton. Fiskerton was little more than a scattering of pleasant houses along the side of the Trent, where a ferry crossed to East Stoke. There was ideal fishing and some gentle scenery. The house was a modest two-storied brick building with a large garden and orchard. Brother William, with his wife and family of four, moved back to the Queen's. Sister Louisa married Joseph Rene Dufrene, landlord of the Crystal Palace Public House, 37 Clumber Street, Nottingham. Although of obvious French descent, Joe Dufrene was a member of a well-known Nottingham family, which had originally been involved in the lace trade – a lot of Nottingham people, including several cricketers, had emigrated to Calais in the early years of the 19th century, Calais being a centre of the French lace industry, and *vice versa*.

There was an important change on the Trent Bridge Ground. On 20 May the old Inn of William Clarke closed its doors for the last time, and in its stead was a brand new public house; at the same time, the County Club had purchased an extra acre of land at the rear of the 1871 pavilion and were busy with plans for a new, much enlarged edifice on this plot. Shrewsbury was back in time for the great Whitsuntide match with Surrey. The 1885 Notts side showed no alterations from the team which had played such excellent cricket in 1884 and there seemed no reason why the championship title should not be retained. Rain unfortunately prevented play before 4.00 pm on the Bank Holiday. This together with some slow cricket resulted in a drawn match, but despite the weather about 16,000 attended the game. The other great match at Trent Bridge was the County v Rest of England. Although a thoroughly representative team could not be obtained, Notts justified their boldness by an innings victory, with Shrewsbury making 56, the highest score of the match, in two hours ten minutes without a chance.

At the beginning of July Shrewsbury received the double honour of being invited to captain the Players against the Gentlemen at both the Oval and Lord's. This was the highest mark of respect which the authorities could bestow on a professional cricketer. At the Oval, Shrewsbury scored 64 and 34 not out to take the Players to a five-wicket win, and in a low scoring game at Lord's, victory was by four wickets, Shrewsbury making 33 and 12 not out.

A week later at Lord's, Shrewsbury created a handful of new records. Middlesex won the toss and batted, but were bowled out for 128. Notts also struggled and by the close of the first day were 139 for 6 with Shrewsbury 86 not out and Attewell 13 not out. By lunch on the second day the over-night pair had raised the total to 285 for 6, Shrewsbury 157 and Attewell 84; after the interval Attewell was soon dismissed, but the pair had created a new Notts seventh wicket record stand of 177. Walter Wright came and went, but at number ten Alf Shaw joined Shrewsbury in another record stand of 93. When the innings ended at last, Shrewsbury had batted seven hours and 55 minutes for a record 224 not out – it was the highest score made in an important match at Lord's since 1820. Notts went on to win the game by an innings.

The next match, at Hove, was also won by an innings, but neither Shrewsbury or Gunn made much contribution to the victory. Maybe Gunn had his mind on other things. A small advertisement had recently appeared in the national press: 'William Gunn and T. J. Moore, The County British Sports Depot, 14 Carrington Street, Nottingham. Best Goods Only at Reasonable Prices.' The most striking point in the announce-ment was the location of the premises – just up the street from the thriving Shaw and Shrewsbury emporium and just down the street from Richard Daft's. Mr Moore, in fact, had been manager of Richard Daft's shop for eleven years and his resignation was another sign of the slow demise of Daft's business.

Shrewsbury made up for his failure at Hove by hitting a century against Gloucestershire: 'a finer display could not have been witnessed.' Notts gained another innings win. The August Bank Holiday game with Surrey was a very slow battle, and with a little rain assisting was drawn, but 28,628 people went through the turnstiles, which was believed to be a record for an inter-county match in London.

Nottinghamshire's splendid form continued to the close of the summer and with just a single defeat, the county retained the title. The title Shrewsbury now earned was that of England's greatest batsman. He averaged 56.50 for the season and of those who played at all regularly the next best was a mere 44.76 by Surrey's Walter Read, giving Shrewsbury a clear margin.

Shrewsbury's success in 1885 finally moved him from being the equal of England's other major batsmen to a pedestal above his contemporaries. E. H. D. Sewell, who knew Shrewsbury in the last few years of his life, commented: 'And so, little by little, this little man playing a quite different kind of cricket to any of the other Big Noises of his time, perfected his own chosen method; never heeding anything in the shape of advice or an adviser, until he became a kind of legend.'

The method to which Sewell referred was Shrewsbury's back-play. Whilst most of the batsmen of the 1870s and 1880s relied on playing off the front foot, Shrewsbury concentrated on playing back, watching the ball until the moment of impact. This enabled him to master the bad wickets which were still very frequently found even on county grounds. William Caffyn, the old Surrey cricketer, pointed out: 'Shrewsbury has always been the master of the grand secret of playing a totally different game when on a hard wicket to when on a soft or sticky one.' This ability, in Caffyn's view, was the hallmark of a really great batsman.

Shrewsbury, who was never a very strong, muscular man, stated that he did not hit the ball, rather that he steered or stroked the ball in the desired direction. He played as if his bat was part of himself. His attitude was unconstrained and perfectly graceful, while every swing and motion of the bat proclaimed the polished expositor of the fine art of cricket.

For the next decade he was the most accomplished batsman in England and even in his forties, with a new generation coming forward, many critics still regarded Shrewsbury as without an equal. Having said that, the question now arises as to the ability of Shrewsbury in comparison with W. G. Grace. The two were totally different in every way, both physically and mentally. Grace's career began more than ten years before Shrewsbury, and the Gloucestershire's cricketer's success was immediate. For 14 successive summers commencing 1868 he was top or thereabouts of the batting averages; allied to his stature as a bowler, this made Grace the colossus he was. By the mid-1880s therefore, everyone accepted that W. G. Grace was the greatest cricketer of all time and so long as he appeared in first-class cricket – his career had another twenty years to run – any comment regarding a possible rival was qualified by a rider which excluded W. G. Grace from the comparison. It is however quite fair to state that during the decade commencing 1885, Shrewsbury was England's best batsman despite the presence of the Grand Old Man.

In November 1885, Shaw and Shrewsbury published a book giving an account of the 1884/5 tour to Australia. The book, costing one shilling, was most comprehensive and well-produced and ran to 190 pages. It is today very much a collector's item. The book was rather late in appearing and perhaps its arrival was connected with the fact that Lillywhite, Shaw and Shrewsbury were in the process of planning a third tour of Australia for 1886/7.

Having fallen out with John Conway, the trio asked J. P. Tennent, who had played for Victoria, to act as their agent. The plans went slowly ahead during the winter of 1885/6, and in the spring several professionals announced that they

Portrait of Arthur Shrewsbury.

The Nottinghamshire team of 1875. *From left to right* Standing: W. Shrewsbury, S. Biddulph, T. Nixon (umpire), Martin McIntyre, R. Daft, J. West (umpire), J. C. Shaw, J. Selby, F. Wild. On the ground: F. Morley, A. Shrewsbury.

The team which went to the USA in 1879. *From left to right* Back row: E. Browne (secretary), F. Morley, G. Ulyett, G. Pinder, W. Oscroft, W. Barnes, R. Daft, J.P. Ford. Front row: E. Lockwood, A. Shrewsbury, W. Bates, J. Selby, A. Shaw, T. Emmett.

Alfred Shaw photographed in San Francisco during the 1881/2 tour.

Arthur Shrewsbury (standing) with his brother William, taken
in about 1880.

William Shrewsbury (1854–1931), taken in about 1900.

THIS TESTIMONIAL IS PRESENTED TO

ARTHVR SHREWSBVRY

together with a PURSE containing Seventy-Two sovereigns in recognition of his wonderful batting average namely - 78.15 for the season of 1887.

His total number of runs in First Class Matches amounted to 1653 for twenty one completed innings; which included eight three figured scores varying from 101 to 267.

This Presentation is further intended to recognise not only Arthur Shrewsbury's great ability as a cricketer, but also his straightforward and honorable conduct, which has won him universal respect both in his Native County and throughout the Cricketing World.

The following Noblemen and Gentlemen residents of the Town and County of Nottingham have subscribed to this Testimonial by a uniform subscription of Five shillings each.

His Grace the Duke of St Albans	Henry Smith Wright M.P.
His Grace the Duke of Portland	Arnold Morley M.P.
The Right Honorable Lord Belper	The Worshipful the Mayor, Ald. Renals
The Very Rev'd the Dean of Rochester	The Sheriff of Nottingham, J. Robinson Esq
Sir Henry Bromley, Bart	J. Turney Esq Ex Mayor of Nottingham

The illuminated address presented to Arthur Shrewbury in 1888 by the Mayor of Nottingham.

SCORES OVER 100

ENGLAND v M.C.C.	152
PLAYERS v GENTN.	111
NOTTS v MIDDLESEX	119
„ v LANCASHIRE	130
„ v SUSSEX	101
„ v GLOSTER	119
„ v MIDDLESEX	267
„ v SUSSEX	135

1887.

A. GOATER, PRINTER, NOTTINGHAM, ENGLAND.

188

A postcard of Arthur Shrewsbury, taken in the 1880s.

had signed contracts to go with the trio. Then came the arrival in England of the 1886 Australians, managed by Major B. J. Wardill of the Melbourne Club. He announced that the Melbourne Club would be financing an English Team to tour Australia and that he would soon be offering contracts to suitable cricketers, both professional and amateur. Many column inches were then filled with the merits of the Melbourne Club's right to sponsor a team as against the rights of Lillywhite, Shaw and Shrewsbury. Major Wardill, in a desperation attempt to win the day, asked the MCC to select his team, but the MCC remained aloof and eventually, though not until August, the Melbourne Club withdrew, leaving the field clear for the trio.

The previews of the 1886 season commenced on rather a bitter note for Nottinghamshire. It was announced that Frank Shacklock would play for the county. Shacklock had appeared for Derbyshire in 1884 and 1885, being born at Crich in that county, but he had lived in Nottinghamshire since the age of six. Under the qualification rules he was entitled to choose at the beginning of each season whether he wished to play for Derbyshire or Notts. Derbyshire were a very weak county and Shacklock no doubt thought he would prosper better at Trent Bridge. As he was Derbyshire's most promising young bowler, this naturally upset Derbyshire supporters. He gained an immediate place in the 1886 Notts side and played regularly that summer, the team being otherwise unchanged. The greed of the Notts Committee at securing the services of Shacklock was to rebound upon the county a few years later, because a promising young Notts colt of 1886 was squeezed out of the side and quickly changed his allegiance to Surrey – the colt was the future England all-rounder, W. H. Lockwood. That however was well into the future. In 1886 the triumphal progress of Notts and of Shrewsbury's batting continued almost without interruption.

The new pavilion was partially opened for the Easter Colts Match and about 9,000 attended, enjoying some unseasonal weather. The game was dominated by two very stout innings – the colt William Harris, from Kimberley, hit 40 in three

hours, whilst Scotton's 80 took nearly five hours. The Australians began Notts' first-class programme, but rain ruined
the match. The Australians, whether due to Lillywhite's plea
or not, were considerably altered from the combination of
1884 under Murdoch, which caused so much ill-feeling. A
report in the magazine *Cricket* noted: 'Very good things are
coming, and very good men, the Australians. They are on
their way hither, and the cricketing spirit flies to greet them
ere they land. This is the first Colonial team that has visited
us since that other gallant body of Colonists was ranged beneath our flag in the Soudan. That is one reason why the
cricketers should be heartily welcomed and hospitably received. Their trip, let us hope, will be free from the usual
dismal squabbles about gate money, about amateur and professional rank, about the distinctions of "Mr" and "Esquire".
The term is under new management and is organised on new
and non-mercenary principles. They will be bad cricketers
who make mountains out of petty mole-hills, social or financial.'

Three Test matches were played, all three being defeats for
Australia. Shrewsbury had a hand in each, but his greatest
innings came in the Lord's match. England, captained by the
Lancashire amateur A. G. Steel, won the toss and decided to
bat, but after thirty minutes play rain caused an interruption
of over an hour and made the wicket ideal for the bowlers.
W. G. Grace, who had opened the batting with Will Scotton,
was dismissed soon after play resumed. This brought Shrewsbury to the crease and the Notts pair added fifty, before Scotton was bowled by Garrett. Walter Read and Steel both fell
cheaply, so that the score was 119 for 4 when Billy Barnes
joined Shrewsbury. The pair defied the attack until close of
play, when the score had reached 202 for 4, Shrewsbury 91,
Barnes 28. On the second day, the Notts batsmen took the
total to 280 and their partnership to 161, then Barnes was
dismissed by Garrett. None of the other England batsmen
achieved much and Shrewsbury was the last to leave, having
batted five minutes under seven hours for 164. The main
editorial note in *Cricket* stated: 'Arthur Shrewsbury's magni-

ficent innings this week is eminently gratifying to those who believe in the survival of the fittest. Shrewsbury has been for the last two years undoubtedly the best professional batsman in the Country, and therefore his brilliant achievement in the great contest of the season, and against the Australian bowling, cannot fail to be particularly satisfactory to all who value the maintenance of our reputation on the cricket-field.'

This innings was only one of three great performances within the space of three weeks. Leading Notts, in the absence of Shaw, against Gloucestershire at Moreton-in-Marsh, Shrewsbury hit 227 not out, carrying his bat through the completed Notts second innings, and staying 465 minutes. With Gunn he added 261 for the second wicket. He thus created a new record individual score for both himself and for Notts. His innings contained two chances, but was not the equal of his 164 at Lord's, since the Gloucester bowling was decidedly moderate. The third of his noted scores was 127 for the Players against the Gentlemen at the Oval. Again the bowling was rather weak which detracted from his fine display.

Nottinghamshire went through the summer undefeated, having seven wins and seven draws. They therefore took the championship title for the fourth successive year. Shrewsbury again headed both the Notts and the first-class batting averages. In the latter table he and Walter Read were the only batsmen to have an average of about 40 and appear regularly in county cricket.

The task of organising the tour to Australia with the competition from Major Wardill and the Melbourne Club did not seem to effect Shrewsbury's cricket. The team for the third Lillywhite, Shaw and Shrewsbury expedition was: W. Barnes, W. Gunn, W. H. Scotton, W. Flowers, M. Sherwin all of Notts, J. Briggs and R. G. Barlow of Lancashire, G. A. Lohmann and Maurice Read of Surrey and W. Bates of Yorkshire, with the three promoters. Shaw and Lillywhite did not intend to take an active role in the matches, which meant the side effectively had only eleven players. The team left Plymouth aboard the Orient steamer *Cuzco* on Saturday 18 September.

The extant letters written by Shrewsbury commence with this voyage and continue almost until his death. Although most of the 300 or so letters are mainly confined to his business activities, they also contain many notes and comments on cricketing matters and thus provide his own feelings and descriptions of events.

There is an unsolved mystery contained in the first batch of letters up to Christmas 1886, for five of them are simply addressed to 'Dear L.' and close with the initials 'T.D.' The recipient is obviously a lady of whom Shrewsbury was very fond, but there is no clue as to her name or address. The main beneficiary in Shrewsbury's will was Gertrude Scott, but it would seem most unlikely to be her. Shrewsbury never married.

The cricketers had a rough passage through the Bay of Biscay, Shrewsbury writes: 'As was to be expected several of our team were unwell for two or three days at first. Amongst the worst by a long way being Gunn, although Barlow, Lillywhite, Briggs, Bates, Read and myself have been far from well and consequently have been absent from the dinner table on more than one occasion. Gunn talked of leaving the ship at Naples, as he said he could not stand the journey, but of course now that he is all right he don't think anything of the kind. It was like a transformation scene, seeing him being led about one day and the following day dancing, romping and singing about the deck, having forgotten all about being ill. Sherwin, as per usual, has been the life and soul of the team, causing a lot of fun by his antics and songs.'

The ship's first port of call was Naples, and having stopped there meant problems in Egypt: 'We are now in quarantine on account of our hitching at Naples where cholera prevails. We have not the slightest illness on board, and it is very strange to me to see the yellow flag flying at the mast head, to denote that no one is allowed to board us. The pilot would not even board us and our big ship had to follow his small boat into safe anchorage. I think it is Port Said which should be quarantined, and not us. We take in 600 or 800 tons of coal here, also an immense quantity of dried fruit (450 tons)

for the colonials' Christmas plum puddings and other neces-
saries for Christmas festivities. There is a boat with a quantity
of Maltese lace, cigars, cigarettes and Turkish delights for sale,
the cigarettes being bought rapidly at 2/- per hundred, the
quality being pretty good (so I am informed). I recognise the
half Frenchman who is disposing of the lace, as the party
whom I, more than once, have had to drive a hard bargain
with. Will try and obtain an interview with him when we
return, all being well. They are not allowed to handle the
coin that is sent down to them in a basket before it has been
pitched into a tin with water in, as a kind of disinfectant.
Some of the lace appears to be very beautiful, but excessive
in price. We have plenty of good singing among our own
fellows each night after dinner and so by that means the
nights pass pretty quickly on. Bath each morning at eleven,
with a little gentle exercise afterwards. Aboard ship life is not
very pleasant, you have a great deal too much idle time in
your hands, which you don't know what to do with. The
living is first class, as good as any hotel (barring tea and
coffee, which I think is caused by the water) but then you
require something to work that off again.... We are now
steaming slowly through the canal at the rate of 5 or 6 knots
an hour. In some parts of the canal the speed is limited to 4
knots an hour.'

A few days later, the ship was sailing through the Red Sea:
'Since leaving Suez we have had a calm sea but the weather
has been unusually hot, in fact more so than I ever experienced before. The chief steward, who has crossed 17 times,
said he never experienced anything like it. In our cabin the
heat registered 96 degrees, in the daytime it was more and in
the sun it would be about 160 degrees. This was on Sunday
and two following days. We no doubt have had it as hot
before but this time a slight breeze was blowing in the same
direction as the boat at the same power. The chief steward
and many of his men could not stand the excessive heat and
consequently have been unable to attend to their duties ...
For two days and nights it has been a continual Turkish bath,
perspiration coming out of every pore in your body and

under-clothing being always wet through. There have been two deaths, a child yesterday and an old woman of over eighty this morning, both of which have been duly confined to the deep. All the team are in first class health. We commence our long run from Aden to Adelaide (6,135 miles) tomorrow, which should take us about 22 days – shall then see our programme of matches. We played cricket last Saturday, eight or nine a-side and shall resume when the temperature is more favourable.'

Conditions however caused Shrewsbury to write eighteen days later: 'Encountered head winds for 8 or 9 days, which made the ship pitch a great deal and caused sea sickness. Ought not to have had more than two days of this weather, which is usual. This will delay our reaching Adelaide until late on Friday next (Oct 29th) or early the following Saturday. Should have been there Thursday with favourable weather. Last week we had sports and concert, our fellows obtaining all the chic prizes. These helped to pass the time away. Am getting tired of the journey, although, looked back upon, it don't seem long since we left Plymouth. Can't say at present whether we stop to play at Adelaide, but if so, am certain to have to go direct from boat to ground, as the match is sure to commence on Saturday the 30th. We have had plenty of cricket on board, but this is not like playing on turf.'

The ship anchored at 5 o'clock on Friday afternoon. The reception arranged at Adelaide Town Hall was abandoned, but at 10 o'clock the following morning the English team was practising in the nets and soon after 12 o'clock the match began. Shrewsbury won the toss and opened the batting. He hit exactly a hundred before being dismissed, though he was lucky in the early stages of his innings. It was however a remarkable effort by someone who had just spent six weeks on the ocean. The match was played in glorious weather, which helped the batsmen, and the result was a draw. Barely 2,000 watched over the three days, which was rather depressing.

The new railway line enabled the team to travel from Ade-

laide to Melbourne, though they had to stop for six hours at
Border Town and another two hours at Dimboola en route.
They stayed at the White Hart, which like the rest of Melbourne was crammed with visitors because of the Melbourne
Cup. The game against Victoria was another high scoring
draw. About 20,000 attended the match, which was marred
by an injury to Shrewsbury, preventing him batting both at
Melbourne and the next stop, Parramatta. On the evening of
13 November, the team arrived at the Oxford Hotel in Sydney,
where Shrewsbury collected his mail from England. The next
day he wrote to his sister Amelia: 'Am glad to hear all are
well at home. You no doubt would be pleased with your trip
to Eccles and I am certain Uncle and Aunt would do all they
possibly could to make both of you comfortable. Am sending
uncle papers each week. Pleased you did not forget to remember me to the frequenters of the bar (of the Queen's Hotel),
do so again and tell them I am well and hearty now. Whilst
playing in our first match at Melbourne I had the misfortune
to split the webb between my little and next finger on my
right hand, when their last man was batting in their first
innings. Felt very much annoyed, as the wicket was a splendid one and the bowling not very strong. It got worse for
some time instead of better, although the doctor told me not
to disturb the lint he had bound it with. It got inflamed and
very hot. I only began to use hot water in time to prevent me
having a bad hand. Am glad to say it is almost better and I
shall make another start against NSW on Friday next. Yesterday I, along with the rest of the team, went down to the
ground to practise and during the afternoon the Governor,
Lord Carrington, came down (he had previously sent us word
he was coming and wished to be introduced to each member
of the team) and was duly introduced to the players. He is a
very nice man and very popular out here. He promised to
visit the match each day. Lady Carrington is coming down
from the mountains purposely for the match. You can't
imagine what amount of good this will do us, as wherever
they go, the people flock to see them. The Australian team
have gone to New Zealand – people say to get out of our way.

Am sending you a Christmas card. Kindly remember me to all at home. With kind love, Your affectionate brother, Arthur Shrewsbury.'

In the New South Wales match, the tourists met Turner and Ferris in partnership for the first time on a rain-affected pitch and were dismissed for under a hundred in both innings – New South Wales batted slightly better to win by 6 wickets. The presence of the Governor meant that 14,000 attended on the second day – the game lasted only two days.

Having two days to spare, Shrewsbury began his rounds of the sports outfitters in Sydney and then wrote to S. Richardson, the manager of Shaw and Shrewsbury's shop in Nottingham: 'Dear Sir, Your two letters with newspapers, the former dated Sept 24th and Oct 8th received here yesterday (Nov 23rd). I have carefully read through the contents of same and noted all particulars. Re: Ball making. I should imagine this is a step in the right direction, if you can clearly show a profit as stated. At the same time you don't want to plunge or act hastely in the matter. Before definitely taking any steps in the matter, be fully convinced that your calculations are correct. This will apply also to the making of leg guards or any other goods. You can't act too cautiously. Should not go to any large outlay, but get into the business by degrees. Mr Woodham (a cricket ball maker in Kent) himself would no doubt be willing to give you some sound information. We want to make a cricket ball that will stand the knocking about as much as Duke's. The balls we send out here are not sufficiently hard. Of course you can make a ball too hard. The sample ball I brought away, which was sent to the shop by some new firm, I tested in our match against NSW and found it first class and also retained its shape. If we could make as good a ball in all particulars as Duke's, we should in time sell as large a quantity as he does, but it is not the slightest use introducing a ball that is an inferior one to knock a better one out. It is very, very difficult to persuade cricketers out here to use any other balls than Duke's. Martin's balls appear to be going fairly well out here. It is on account of their hard nature.

Electric Light would be a great advantage if as cheap and you could rely upon the supply being regular.

Lock up Shop, Scarcely like the idea, as it would entail a rather heavy additional expense and I think we ought to be able in our present place of business (now that we manufacture) to sell some cheap lines, as well as better quality. If we can only once get a name for Tennis, we can then do a large trade, but to do this you must keep some cheap quality bats.

Re: Salary – this must remain as at present.'

The letter continued by naming half-a-dozen sports goods firms which Shrewsbury had visited and making comments on each regarding possible orders and the right man to contact in each firm. Shrewsbury took on his rounds samples and catalogues, but almost all the Australian firms ordered through their London agents.

After four odds matches, the team returned to Sydney for the return against New South Wales. This time Ferris and Turner were not so deadly and as the home batting collapsed twice, the tourists won by nine wickets. Shrewsbury's 64 was easily the best score of the match. On Friday about 3,000 attended, but the presence of Lord Carrington on Saturday boosted the figure that day to about 10,000.

Shrewsbury's sister Amelia wrote to ask his opinion regarding the possible sale of the Queen's Hotel. Arthur replied that it could not be sold at a profit and that the reason business was slack was the slump in the lace trade, which would probably soon ease. His lady-friend also wrote and from Arthur's reply she was complaining of boredom: 'No doubt you would thoroughly enjoy yourself at the Goose Fair, I know you would have done had I been present. Am speaking for myself (when I say) madame ought to go out more frequently, and I don't see anything to prevent it. The wedding you speak of would liven you up a little and cause you to think of happier times of the past. You being busy at the house will cause time to slip along. I intended going to see Mr Barry Sullivan at the Nottingham Theatre before I left home, had he visited there, but I think he came about the week following. We have a Mr and Mrs Sheridan here performing Shakespeare pieces and they are thought a great deal of, but in my humble opinion, are not to be compared to the acting of Barry Sullivan in Louis XI. (Note: Barry Sullivan, well-known actor-manager, died in 1891 aged 69; the play Louis XI by Dion Boucicault was first performed in London in 1855 and revived several times up to 1910.) Our team is trying to organise a Minstrel Troupe so as to give an entertainment at various up-country places we play at. I think judging from present appearances this will fall through ... You speak about not seeing me again – I hope and trust you will many times yet. The paper I write on is for the purpose of keeping a copy of what I send you, so that no dispute may occur afterwards as to the number and the purport of each letter. Just to show what a variety of entertainment they possess here, an earthquake occurred at the place we were playing, at about 3 or 4 o'clock in the morning and shook some of our fellows out of their beds. Was told afterwards this earthquake was got up purposely for our amusement. Was fortunate enough not to hear it, as I was fast asleep – sleeping the sleep of the innocent.'

As a partner in the family lace firm, Shrewsbury did the rounds of the various Sydney shops which sold Nottingham lace. He was fortunate enough to be introduced to the prospective Mayor of Sydney, Mr Riley, who took Shrewsbury round a number of wholesale houses. As with sports goods he found that all orders were made through London agents. He wrote home to brother Joe with a list of firms and their agents commenting: 'Lace has been sold here in large quantities, but it is chiefly German and has knocked the Nottingham manufacturers into a cocked hat.' The Shrewsbury firm did not produce the finished product and Arthur found that presentation – a fancy box and lace which would display well – stole the market.

A few days later came a letter of the lady-friend in reply to the one Arthur had posted at the beginning of the tour. She complained that her letter bore a striking resemblance to those received by Arthur's family. Shrewsbury wrote back: 'Should have had nothing to report to other people if I had not sent them a repetition of what I sent you. Of course the private part of the business was left out. The prepared paper I use can supply me with five copies at once. You will readily see what a reduction in labour that is (don't laugh). This letter as you particularly requested is original and addressed only to you. You may have heard me speak about a boat out here called the Helen Nicoll, which we re-christened the Billy Nickoll. All our fellows remember her only too well on account of the fearful time they spent aboard her. (On the 1884/5 tour.) You will see by the cutting enclosed that she has been in a collision. Am not at all surprised at this, as the captain was always playing cards and actually, when all of us were sick, stopped the engines to see if he could catch some fish. We have not forgiven him for this.'

Shrewsbury's business dealings in Sydney kept him occupied longer than he expected and he therefore travelled to Melbourne the day after the remainder of the team. The Australian side had returned from New Zealand; the stage was therefore set for the first big match in Melbourne against the Australian side selected by the Melbourne Club. The game proved a splendidly fought affair with the advantage being gained by first one side and then the other and the tourists, though following on, won in the end by 57 runs. Shrewsbury hit 38 and 62, the highest aggregate in the match. Rain interfered with Saturday's play and the attendance over the five days was very poor – only 800 on Saturday, 2,000 on the first day, 2,500 on the third and under 2,000 on the fourth and fifth – a great disappointment to the promoters.

Under the surface of amicability between the Melbourne Club and the English side there was the undercurrent of distrust which stemmed from Shrewsbury managing to outwit Wardill when the latter wished to bring a team to Australia. In the middle of the Melbourne match, Shrewsbury wrote to his brother Joe: 'You no doubt will have seen our cablegram in the papers announcing we are coming out here next year. This is correct and we have the support of the Sydney Trustees, and what is more important, we have secured the Sydney Ground, where the money is made. The Melbourne Club want to bring out a team, but we have checkmated them to such a degree that they are perfectly furious over it and swear they will also bring a team. We don't care if they do, they can't play at Sydney and they will be cutting their own throats if they go on with it. They caused us a great deal of trouble and expense when in England over the team we have here and so we are trying to pay them back in their own coin.'

From his base at the White Hart Hotel in Burke Street, Melbourne, Shrewsbury did the rounds of both the sports goods shops and the firms dealing with lace. He discovered that the leading Nottingham firm, Thos Adams and Co, did some £10,000 worth of business in Melbourne each year and the firm's salesman was George Royle, the old Notts amateur cricketer, who had captained the Lace Team in 1872, when Shrewsbury had made his debut in the match against the Hosiery side.

The team left Melbourne for Geelong and Ballarat. At the former Shrewsbury and Scotton added 147 for the first wicket. The match was drawn and the attendance appalling, about 300 on each day. In Ballarat spectators were more numerous – 4,000 and 3,000 plus 1,000 on the third day. Shrewsbury visited the local sports emporium and found that F. H. Ayres, the London firm, were doing good business and that Warsop's bats were undercutting the rest of the market. He wrote to Mr Richardson on these matters and continued: 'Enclosed you will find agreement for Puffer (this is not the correct spelling of his name, but the way it is pronounced) of Leicestershire to sign for next year to come out with us if selected. You can offer him in all £180 or £200 and even go as high as £220, if he won't sign for less. I don't think Preston of Yorks would sign again as last time if selected, and we don't wish to engage him permanently yet. ... Trust everything is going on satisfactory at Business. We are coming home in a P and O boat and will send you particulars later on. P.S. I was having a little practice yesterday with a Barfleet bat with very little wood in it, but the Patent Handle made it drive beautifully, you ought to examine one and see if we can't adopt an improved principle, the spring saves the blade a great deal.' (Note: Puffer is A.D. Pougher, who did go with the 1887/8 side, as did J.M. Preston.) Shrewsbury was attempting to sign up the leading professionals for the 1887/8 tour before the Melbourne Club agent could do so.

Following the two up-country games, the tourists returned to Melbourne for the most important match there, the fixture played over the New Year. The opposition was again the Melbourne Club's Australian Team. The home side led by Garrett won the toss and batted. They did not make best use of a good wicket and some terrible running between the wickets cost them dear. The wicketkeeper, Blackham, saved the day with 63. Shrewsbury badly injured a finger when fielding and could not open the English innings. Wickets fell quickly and Shrewsbury came in for some criticism when he eventually went in to bat at number ten. He and Sherwin added 49 for the last wicket to take England into the lead by 30 runs. In the second innings the Australians struggled for six hours to make 249 and this left 210 minutes for England to score 220, the game having to end at 4.10 so the cricketers could catch the express to Sydney. The match was drawn. Both teams then assembled on the Association Ground for the third match. The English side gained a decisive first innings lead in this game, a fact which detracted from the interest on the third and fourth days, so that the total attendance was about 16,000, the same as at Melbourne the previous week. At this stage of the tour it should have been obvious to the promoters that the crowds were not as big as in 1884/5 and the tour would not bring much of a profit, and yet they were pushing ahead with plans for 1887/8. On the face of it the object of the 1887/8 projected tour was simply to do down the Melbourne Club, since there would be little financial gain. One is forced to the conclusion that this attitude was mainly Shrewsbury's. In the final analysis neither Shaw or Lillywhite had the stamina for what amounted almost to a vendetta – judging by their normal behaviour they were keen on an easy life.

Four up-country matches followed the Sydney game. This

short programme was marred by rain. A continuous down-
pour for nine days in some parts caused tremendous damage.
The weather however improved for a prompt start to be made
to the match against Combined Australia – unfortunately the
Sydney morning papers carried the rumour that the game
was postponed twenty-four hours, and thus few spectators
turned up. Shrewsbury wrote this account to his sister, Amelia: 'We have just finished a match against the Combined
Team of Australia and I don't think that during the time I
have played cricket, I ever played in a match that was literally
pulled out of the fire, as this one was. It was so entirely
unexpected that the people out here could scarcely realise
that we had won. It was a glorious victory and I am sure the
cricket public at home will be more than pleased with the
result, considering the up-hill game we had to fight. All our
players during the Combined last innings worked and fielded
like a high machine, every man thinking it was on their
individual efforts the result of the match depended. I shall
never forget the shout our players gave when Lohmann
bowled the last man (Spofforth) out and the groan of disappointment that arose from the spectators. I am sorry to say
that some of the players did not take their defeat as gracefully
as we should have liked, saying that our umpire (Rawlinson
of Yorks, an old experienced umpire) had given two bad decisions. I won't enter into what further was said, but should
wish that Colonial Teams could bear licking with the same
graceful manner as they can a win.' In this match Australia
were set 111 to win in the final innings and were dismissed
for 97 with Billy Barnes taking 6 for 28. Barnes was then
involved in a fight with the Australian batsman, McDonnell.
Barnes, in attempting to punch McDonnell, struck the wall
and so injured his fist that he was unable to play for almost
the rest of the tour.

Nine thousand turned up on the second day – Saturday, but
with low scores the match was all over on the third afternoon. Shrewsbury noted: 'We are having very poor gates and
I am sadly afraid that it will take us all our time to pay
expenses. I think our side is too good and cricket has mater-

ially gone down especially in Victoria. Novelty is what is
required out here. Pain's fireworks attracted 20 or 30 thousand people in one night and the following nights immense
crowds have witnessed his fireworks.'

Following the great victory, the team had a difficult journey
by train and steamer to Narrabri for a game sponsored by a
local landowner, Mr Moseley, who had prepared horses so
that the team could go kangaroo hunting – only Scotton and
Briggs went. The match was not taken too seriously and lots
were drawn to decide the batting order – Shrewsbury went
in at number ten and helped Flowers add 127 for the ninth
wicket. Matches at Newcastle, Armidale and Singleton
followed. On returning to Sydney the tourists met the New
South Wales team and were completely overwhelmed by
C. T. B. Turner, Shrewsbury having the dubious honour of
being bowled without scoring in both innings by the 'Terror',
the first time he had ever bagged a pair. The wicket was
difficult throughout with none of the team totals reaching
200, and of course the English team lacked Barnes. Immediately following this defeat came another match at Sydney
against Combined Australia. Shrewsbury was again twice dismissed by Turner for 9 and 6 and generally the English batting was poor. Happily George Lohmann shot out the Australians for 84 and in another low scoring affair the tourists
won by 71 runs.

The rivalry between the Melbourne Club and Shrewsbury
was further extended by the New South Wales Cricket
Association. Shrewsbury had the agreement with the Sydney
Trustees regarding the use of their ground for 1887/8 and
Melbourne then approached the NSWCA for assistance in
carrying out the plans for their 1887/8 team, but the
NSWCA were at pains to point out that they had no control
over the Sydney Ground and had to pay the Trustees for the
use of it.

The English team went to Melbourne on 3 March and after
a day at the races began a final game against Victoria.
Shrewsbury made up for his disappointing scores in Sydney:
'No praise could be too much for the magnificent play of

Shrewsbury; all the bowlers were alike to him, as he played them with the most consummate ease.' He hit 144. The tourists won by nine wickets, but the crowds were very thin, not much over 5,000 in four days.

There were two odds matches before the famous Smokers v Non-Smokers game was staged on the East Melbourne Ground. The English team and the best Victorian players divided into two elevens for this game. Shrewsbury opened the batting with Bruce and the pair added 195 for the first wicket, Bruce being lbw to Palmer. Bates went cheaply, then Gunn and Shrewsbury added 311 for the third wicket, a new first-class record. Shrewsbury was eventually out for 236, with 40 fours. The run feast continued but it was largely ignored by the public, who preferred to go to a bicycle race staged on the Melbourne Ground. At East Melbourne less than 1,000 turned out each day and on the last day only 100.

The team took the express train direct from Melbourne to Adelaide, the journey taking eighteen hours, and played their final match against Fifteen of South Australia. Less than 1,500 watched during the three days. Sailing from Adelaide on 27 March, the team arrived in Colombo on 10 April and spent two days there, finally landing at Plymouth on 8 May.

Shrewsbury's batting was the great success of the tour. In first-class games and in all games he was the only player to exceed an average of 30 and the following comment on his other strengths was reported: 'His fielding was at all times brilliant at point and as a captain he must be considered very good, being watchful to note the weak points of his opponents.'

As had been several times forecast, the team did not make a profit, this being due to poor crowds in Melbourne and the lack of interest in the Melbourne Club Australian Team, which opposed the tourists in three major matches.

6 Jubilee Year

At the end of March 1887 a long article appeared in the *Melbourne Telegraph* written by Shrewsbury. He stated that the New South Wales cricketers were much better than those of Melbourne, because the former had the opportunity to play on all types of wicket, whereas at Melbourne the wickets favoured the batsman. Although he condemned batsmen who were purely defensive, he was equally critical of those who threw caution to the winds and took chances in order to score runs quickly. On two new ideas he showed his disapproval. He did not think that six-ball overs would improve cricket, nor did he approve of the idea of counting maiden overs to the credit of the fielding side. In connection with the 1887/8 tour he commented: 'A Sydney gentleman has guaranteed us against any loss. We shall have a very strong eleven – better than 1886/7 – and this is the best which has ever been in Australia far and away.'

Meanwhile the NSW Cricket Association had received a cablegram from the Melbourne Club asking if they would combine to sponsor a team to Australia in 1887/8. They claimed to have signed up Walter Read, Roller, Hawke, Walker, Stoddart, Vernon, possibly Studd and were negotiating with W. G. Grace. The NSWCA replied that it did not feel inclined to take any part in the proposals.

Before disbanding entirely, the 1886/7 team travelled to Glasgow where they played Sixteen of West of Scotland in a two-day game. Shrewsbury on his reappearance at home was leg before without scoring. The serious cricket began at Trent Bridge on Whit Monday.

The principal alteration in the Notts side at the start of the

1887 season was the removal of Alfred Shaw as captain and the appointment of Mordecai Sherwin. Shrewsbury was invited to take Shaw's place, but declined, whether out of sympathy with Shaw or another reason is not clear. Shaw was very upset by his dismissal and it was later to appear that the Notts Committee had been too precipitous in their action, even though he was now in his 45th year.

Although the match with Surrey was the first Notts game of the summer, it was described in retrospect as the match of the season. Surrey gained a first innings lead of 26 and through Walter Read and Roller took their second innings total to 264 for 5, at which point Shuter, the Surrey captain, ordered his batsmen to throw away their wickets. Notts ended with 316 needed but not sufficient time to make them and could only play for a draw. Only William Gunn however played with any conviction and Surrey won with 30 minutes in hand – it was the first time in 26 years that Surrey had beaten Notts at Trent Bridge and curiously the only time in 1887 that Shrewsbury failed to make a substantial contribution to the Notts totals.

Notts' first away game was at Lord's. For once Middlesex were able to field a fairly representative eleven, but Shrewsbury opened with an excellent 119 and some good bowling by Dick Attewell provided Notts with an innings victory. In the Yorkshire match at Trent Bridge runs came so painfully slowly that in three days only 700 were scored, of which Shrewsbury made 81, the highest on either side for the second match in succession. He repeated this feat against Lancashire, hitting 130 and Notts attained an innings victory.

Prior to this he made 152 for England v MCC at Lord's in the match to celebrate the centenary of the premier club. With Stoddart he added 266 for the first wicket. It was the highest opening stand recorded in an important match at Lord's; Shrewsbury was at the wicket five hours and a quarter without giving a chance. Shrewsbury went on to score another hundred in the Gentlemen v Players game at Lord's, when he led the Players to an innings victory.

Though he failed in the repeat fixture at the Oval, Shrewsbury scored 24 and 74 not out for Notts against Kent, taking his county to a nine-wicket win. At Hove he helped Scotton in an opening partnership of 172, Shrewsbury being the first man out for 101, and Notts won another innings victory. At this stage of the season both Surrey and Notts had played six matches and each had been beaten once.

G.F. Vernon, the Middlesex amateur, was engaged by the Melbourne Club to sign up players for their 1887/8 touring team, but was having some problems, Bowley and Key of Surrey both declining; he also approached Pougher, who had already been signed by Shrewsbury.

Tremendous crowds turned up at the Oval to watch the August Bank Holiday game, Surrey v Notts, 51,607 paying at the turnstiles. Notts gained a first innings lead of 36, with fortune favouring both camps. First young Henry Richardson, after being dropped, helped Sherwin to add 79 for the last Notts wicket, then Sherwin injured his wrist and was unable to keep while Surrey batted, which resulted in several fielding errors. Notts only made 168 in their second innings, leaving Surrey requiring 205. They achieved their target with four wickets in hand. The GPO delivered no less than 110 telegrams to the Oval asking for the latest score.

Nottinghamshire had beaten a weak Gloucestershire side immediately before their Surrey game. Another Shrewsbury hundred gave Notts the opportunity of inflicting a second innings defeat on Gloucestershire on the College Ground at Clifton. Shrewsbury arrived on the ground to find the match already commenced, so he went in at number five and carried out his bat for 119, and with Frank Shacklock added 146 for the ninth wicket.

In a friendly fixture at Edgbaston, Shrewsbury scored 96 for Notts against Warwickshire, the first match ever played between the two counties. Middlesex then came to Trent Bridge and spent almost two days watching Shrewsbury bat. With Sherwin absent injured, Shrewsbury won the toss and decided to bat on a splendid wicket. With Scotton he added 167 for the first wicket, Scotton then being dismissed for 51.

William Gunn came in at number three, but made only 12 and was replaced by Billy Barnes when the total had reached 189. Barnes and Shrewsbury took the score to 312 for 2 at the close with Shrewsbury 171 and Barnes 66. On the second day, Tuesday, Barnes hit out, whilst Shrewsbury continued on his patient way. The stand reached 214 in 210 minutes when Barnes was bowled by F. G. J. Ford for 115. Shrewsbury was eighth out with the score at 536 and his own score a record 267. He had been at the crease 615 minutes, and the Wisden report noted: 'during the whole of this time he did not give a real chance. Such a thing, we believe, can scarcely have ever been said of an innings lasting so long a period.' It was of course both a new record for Nottinghamshire and for Shrewsbury. It remains to this day the longest innings ever played in a county championship match. Notts innings ended at 6.25 on the second evening with the score at 596. It was before declarations were permitted, and Middlesex batted out the final day.

In complete contrast, Notts then went to Old Trafford, where they were beaten by ten wickets. Shrewsbury and Scotton added 49 for the first wicket, but the entire side were dismissed for 92, Scotton carrying out his bat with 35 not out. They achieved very few more in the second innings. R. G. Barlow and Johnny Briggs were the cause of Notts downfall, the county's third defeat of the season.

From Manchester the team went to Bramall Lane, Sheffield. As was usual, the game against Yorkshire was grimly fought. Notts made 241 on the whole of the first day, with Shrewsbury hitting 75. On the second Yorkshire replied with 214 for 8. Notts collapsed in their second innings and Yorkshire were left needing 119 to win in 95 minutes. The game built up to an exciting climax and when the last ball had been bowled Yorkshire still needed three runs with two wickets in hand.

The arrangements for the two tours to Australia continued to hold the headlines. C. Aubrey Smith was approached both by Vernon and Shrewsbury, but decided to join the latter. W. E. Roller, who had signed for Vernon, had to withdraw due to illness and the Surrey professional, Bobby Abel, was brought in to replace him. It was announced that both teams would sail aboard the Orient steamer *Iberia*, leaving Plymouth on 7 September.

The last Notts home match was against Sussex on 25 August. The visitors were dismissed for 140 and Notts went in to bat at a quarter to five on the first afternoon, Shrewsbury being accompanied by J. A. Dixon. At stumps the score was 91 without loss, Dixon 34, Shrewsbury 48. On the second morning Dixon was dismissed at 109, after which Gunn and Shrewsbury added 181 for the second wicket, Shrewsbury losing his wicket for 135 – he gave only one chance. The score at the close of the second day was 424 for 3. On the last day Notts hit out and were dismissed for 570, with Gunn making 205 not out. Sussex had 3¾ hours batting time, but Notts dismissed them with a few minutes in hand. The fate of the championship was held by Surrey, in that they needed only to avoid defeat to gain the title. This they did and therefore came out top of the table for the first time since 1864.

The final Notts game provided another victory. This time Kent were the victims at Mote Park, Maidstone. In a low scoring match, Shrewsbury made the highest individual score, 53.

Shrewsbury had achieved, by a small margin, the highest average ever attained up to that date in a first-class English season. The details of the leading six batsmen of 1887 are as follows:

	M	I	NO	Runs	HS	Avge	100s
A. Shrewsbury (*Notts*)	17	23	2	1653	267	78·71	8
W. G. Grace (*Gloucs*)	24	46	8	2062	183*	54·26	6
A. J. Webbe (*Middx*)	18	31	5	1244	243*	47·84	3
W. W. Read (*Surrey*)	23	36	2	1615	247	47·50	5
K. J. Key (*OU/Sy*)	24	44	5	1684	281	43·17	2
W. E. Roller (*Surrey*)	10	12	0	490	120	40·83	3

All the other batsmen in the list were amateurs. Lilly-white's Cricketers' Annual for 1888 published Shrewsbury's portrait as a frontispiece and gave a brief summary of his

achievements. Wisden had not introduced its 'Five Cricketers
of the Year' feature, but in the review of Nottinghamshire
cricket commented: 'Undoubtedly the feature of the Notts
season was the marvellously consistent batting of Arthur
Shrewsbury, who has more clearly than ever established his
right to be considered the finest professional bat in England.'

Despite this run glut, the Notts public were not going to
Trent Bridge in as large numbers as in previous years, save
for the Whitsun game. Only an average of 2,000 per day saw
the Yorkshire match and the cause was put down to the very
slow run rate: 'That they carried this policy of careful batting
to excess there can be little doubt; many of the eleven have
probably watched Arthur Shrewsbury's success with envy,
and have tried to copy his method of batting, forgetting that
Shrewsbury always played the same game and always took
a long time to make his runs.' This further note in Wisden of
1888 may have been partially correct, but C.B. Fry a few
years later did not agree with the last sentence: 'Arthur has
been very quiet, and a little monotonous, but somehow or
other he has scored almost as fast as other batsmen who have
come and gone. There was a quick scorer in with him who
notched 61 in just under two hours, while Arthur compiled
52. That makes about 60 runs an hour between them, which
is not very slow scoring. But is not Arthur Shrewsbury the
slowest scorer in England? Wrong; he scores just as fast as
any other batsman who is not a professed hitter. The idea
that he is slow is mistaken. True, he is often half an hour
without getting a run; but somehow he makes up for it and
is all but even with his more mobile partner. It is most decep-
tive. The fact is he waits for the ball he wants, and then
secures a certain fourer. He does not waste time and energy
in banging ball after ball into fieldsmen's hands. He waits and
scores – waits and scores. You see a man go in, open his
shoulders and bustle about; then you say it is fast, free cricket.
Shrewsbury makes no fuss, and you think it slow. This is a
delusion. Runs are coming much at the same pace either
way. If you go into the matter you will find it so.'

If 1887 was the pinnacle of Shrewsbury's long career, the

season was no isolated high point and his domination of the English batting can be shown by the fact that he was the leading batsman each season from 1885 to 1892 inclusive, save for 1888 when he did not play and 1889 when he missed half the season. In the history of first-class cricket only two other batsmen have achieved a similar domination, W. G. Grace in the 1870s and Walter Hammond in the 1930s. Measured against their contemporaries therefore, it would be quite fair to say that after W. G. Grace, Hammond and Shrewsbury share an equal second place.

7 Cricket and Football Tours

The two teams of rival English cricketers left England aboard the Orient steamer, *Iberia*, bound for Australia. Some of the players went on board at Tilbury and the remainder, two days later at Plymouth. The two parties consisted of: C. A. Smith (capt.), G. Brann, L. C. Docker, J. M. Read, A. D. Pougher, G. Ulyett, R. Pilling, G. A. Lohmann, J. M. Preston, J. Briggs, W. Newham with the promoters J. Lillywhite and A. Shrewsbury; and Hon. M. B. Hawke (capt.), G. F. Vernon, A. E. Stoddart, T. C. O'Brien, A. B. Newton, W. W. Read, M. P. Bowden, R. Abel, J. Beaumont, J. T. Rawlin, W. Bates, R. Peel and W. Attewell under the auspices of the Melbourne Club.

Even before they had gained their sea legs, the *Adelaide Observer* fired a salvo: 'It is almost certain that the English amateurs who are to visit Australia under the auspices of the Melbourne Club will play three matches in Adelaide. ... I do not think our Association will fix any matches with the professional team that is to be brought out by Shaw and Shrewsbury. They will have to depend to a great extent upon New South Wales for support.' The publicity of the Melbourne Club had already done its work in Adelaide. The inference from the quoted report is that South Australia was going to play with the nice 'amateurs', but going to ignore the naughty 'professionals'. The fact that both sides were a mixture of amateur and professional talent was neither here nor there.

Philip Sheridan, Managing Trustee of the Sydney Cricket Ground, wrote at length to the press, stating that the Trustees were acting as agents for Shaw and Shrewsbury, but would not indemnify the professionals against any losses, he went on to say that he was unaware of the Melbourne Club's plans at the time the Trustees invited Shaw and Shrewsbury to tour. The Melbourne Club then announced that Sheridan knew perfectly well of the Club's plans before the Trustees invited Shaw and Shrewsbury. The two teams were therefore in very stormy waters before they actually arrived in Australia. Mr Wardill of the Melbourne Club was touring the various country towns trying to arrange fixtures with his English team, before the Sydney agents arrived: 'the showman who gets ahead on the road will probably cut out his opponent', commented the *Sydney Mail*.

The *Iberia* arrived safely in Adelaide on 25 October. On the voyage however Shrewsbury was too busy with the future to concern himself with the present squabbles. He wrote back to Shaw, who remained in Nottingham: 'Re: Football Tour, In the first place keep this matter as private as possible and even when you hear from us to engage players, keep it secret until you have fastened four or five of the principal ones. After that let the Press Association have it. Make the agreements with the players binding only in the event of our bringing a team from England (as per cricket engagement) and if you can, and the players will sign it, put a clause in, binding them not to visit Australia in a Football capacity unless under our joint management. Also enter into agreements with them to play us two or three matches before leaving England, us paying all expenses. ... I think the more Amateurs you obtain the better it will be, at the same time they must be good ones. You must work up the affair and if possible get a banquet up for the team before leaving England.' Shrewsbury then continued with an elaborate code for cables between him and Shaw – the cost of cabling more than two or three words was prohibitive at that time. He ended the letter with: 'You may depend upon it that if the Melbourne Club can give us a slap in the face they will only too readily do it. That is why everything must be completed before it is made public, so that they will be harmless in the matter. Should the football affair be a success, and I am not a bit doubtful about it myself, the Melbourne Club will be sure to try it on the following year and that is the principal reason we shall try and engage the Colonial Grounds for two or three years. And that is why we require a number of Amateurs in our team so as to knock the wind out of the sails of the Melbourne Club. P.S. Let a professional man see that the agreement with the football players is a legal and binding one.'

At the Shaw and Shrewsbury shop, Mr Richardson had been replaced by Mr Sadler as manager. Despite the presence of Alf Shaw, Shrewsbury still tried to run the shop from the *Iberia*. The following letter had the heading the 'Red Sea': 'Make a good show of footballs and have a leading low line. Would not have too many blown up as it injures the pipe in the bladder,' he writes to Sadler. 'We are having it very hot in the Red Sea and to make matters worse, Mr Lillywhite has taken a two-berth inside cabin, where no light of day can permeate and where no fresh air ever comes, it having no port hole. It is simply fearful and it is impossible to sleep in it. Even in cold weather it is a small dreary hole and much the worst cabin I have ever used. I hope you will keep everything in first class order this winter, as I am perfectly certain four times the business can be done with attention. Don't order too great a quantity of any particular class of goods except bat wood. Hoping you and Mrs Sadler are well.'

Whilst the Melbourne Club sponsored team, now known as Vernon's XI, played a four-day game in Adelaide, Shrewsbury's side travelled to Parramatta for a country match to open their programme, a week later.

The team were met at the station by the mayor and other representatives and in blazing weather the locals, having won the toss, elected to bat. Lohmann and Briggs soon dismissed the XVIII of Parramatta and just after lunch Shrewsbury and Ulyett opened the tourists' innings – the report comments at this point: 'the Englishmen opened the eyes of the yokels.' At any rate the pair added 101 for the first wicket, with Shrewsbury batting in the style he had so frequently demonstrated during the late English summer. A first innings lead of 200 was achieved but the game being confined to two days, Parramatta batted out their second innings for a draw. From a financial viewpoint the match was not so satisfactory. Only a thousand attended the first day and much less on the second.

Returning to Sydney, the Englishmen were taken by government launch for a picnic outing, prior to the start of the first major game – against New South Wales. Shrewsbury however stayed at the hotel to catch up with his correspondence. 'I want you to tell Mr Trimmings at the Factory,' he wrote to Mr Sadler, 'to be very careful in putting the handles into the blades and not to drive them down too tightly. The bat I gave Ulyett at Nottingham, one of our patents, was a very good one, the wood being first rate quality ... but during our match with Parramatta it split completely down the centre, which was in my opinion caused by tight splicing. It was a great pity as a more beautiful and better wearing piece of wood could not be found.'

Shrewsbury had brought out to Australia, among other items, a quantity of Shaw and Shrewsbury cricket balls and he used these in the team's matches as an advertisement and was very impressed with their durability, especially the fact that use in wet weather did not seem to affect them. That was one pleasant surprise, but on his rounds of the Sydney sports shops he found other aspects of trade not so bright. He comments to Mr Sadler; 'Mr Killick (a shop manager) complains that he has been charged for 12 dozen sets of stumps instead of 12 sets ... one of the bladders on the inflated boxing gloves has given way, so in future thoroughly test them before sending them out ... You must also contrive to make the bats sent out here a browner colour. They won't have them looking so pale and many a good bat is thrown aside in consequence.'

The match against New South Wales in Sydney was scheduled to begin on Wednesday, but continuous rain forced the authorities to abandon play not only that day, but on Thursday as well. The enforced rest turned Shrewsbury's mind back to the football tour. He cabled the single code word 'Affix' back to Alfred Shaw – meaning start selecting the side at once, and he wrote to say that Shaw should try and sign up a number of amateurs, because they would 'raise the tone of the team' and might be persuaded to come for expenses only. Shrewsbury however seemed not too concerned that the English Rugby players would have to adapt themselves to Victorian Rules Football for many of the important matches. He wrote to Mr Sadler: 'When on board ship the team would have to study the Laws (of the Victorian game), so as to know them thoroughly, in fact off by heart ... Jack Conway has promised to make me out a diagram of a football field, which I will forward ... Am told this morning that there is no off or on side play in the Victorian Rules of Football. This, they say, is where the material difference exists between the Rugby game at home and the game out here. Trusting you are pushing the Business and that trade is steadily improving.'

Thinking over the idea of saving money by employing amateurs, Shrewsbury went a step further when he realised that even more money could be saved by persuading the amateur cricketers already in Australia with the two English teams to stay on and join the football tour. He approached three of his side – Brann, Newham and C. A. Smith – and Stoddart of the Melbourne side. Stoddart was a noted Rugby footballer with Blackheath RFC, but Brann and Smith were more acquainted with soccer. Shrewsbury would immediately save four passages to and from Australia, if these cricketers could be persuaded to stay out.

When the amount of money involved in setting up this football venture is taken into account, the whole conception seems to have been alarmingly haphazard. So far as is known, Shrewsbury himself never played Rugby football and only played soccer at local Nottingham club level in his youth. Back in Nottingham, Alfred Shaw had very little connection with football and the third partner, Lillywhite, also was not connected with the game. Shrewsbury however continued to dispatch advice back to England; 'In the team you are selecting to send out here, some judgement will be required, as we should not require too many three-quarter backs, or too many half or full backs, or too many of any one particular. P.S. It would be no good to bring out a 2nd class team, you must obtain *the very best men* ... Obtain four or five of the very best players in the world and they will advise you who also to secure. I am only giving you this as being my own private opinion, you must exercise your own discretion in the matter. Stoddart and Newham are three-quarter backs, and Brann and Smith would, I think, be useful as forwards.'

Meanwhile, after the two-day postponement, the match against New South Wales started on a sodden wicket. The home team won the toss and put the tourists in to bat. The famous pair of Turner and Ferris opened the bowling and reduced the batsmen to a procession, bar Shrewsbury. The side was all out for 49, but Shrewsbury made 20, playing with 'great care and judgement'. New South Wales struggled to 80 for 7 by stumps. The attendance was good and there was a fair crowd for the second day, when New South Wales' innings soon ended and the English team disintegrated for a second time to Turner who was 'very puzzling on a wicket that suited him to a nicety.' The game was lost by ten wickets.

After a further day in Sydney, the team took the steamer for Brisbane, a voyage of forty-four hours. At that time Queensland cricket was not in any way the equal of Victoria or New South Wales and therefore the three-day game was the English eleven against eighteen of Queensland. The Exhibition Ground, about a mile and a half out of Brisbane, had just been opened and a grandstand built. It was estimated that 20,000 could watch the match – unfortunately for Shrewsbury only a tenth of that number turned out on the first day, despite the presence of the Governor. The locals, batting first, were dismissed for 79. The tourists began badly and were 58 for 5, when Shrewsbury went in to bat. At the close he was still not out and a first innings lead secured. Shrewsbury had made 35 when he was given out 'leg-before wrongly'. His score was, however, the highest of the match and he was therefore required to go to the local theatre to be presented on stage with a cup by the minstrel troupe, then performing in Brisbane. The report noted that Shrewsbury could not be found when called upon for the presentation and appropriately C. A. Smith went on stage and accepted the cup on Shrewsbury's behalf.

Two up-country games – at Maryborough and Gympie – provided the team with two victories against local twenty-twos, before a return game with the eighteen of Queensland. There seemed little interest in cricket in the colony. Even in perfect cricket weather on the Saturday of the return with Queensland only 1,200 turned up and on the Monday the 'crowd' numbered 50.

Shrewsbury toured the sports goods firms of the area and wrote at great length to Shaw explaining the various specialities and personnel of each of the firms he visited. He continued: 'Get all the amateurs and professionals to use our Patent bat next season, even if you have to give them one, or even two each. If business goes on as I expect, you will require more room in the factory. Wish we could get some first class cricket ball makers to make as good a ball as Dukes. Am pushing business all I can out here and feel we shall do a large trade with colonial houses in future. Could not Mr Trimming introduce a new handle for tennis racquets? They like new ideas out here, if they are any good. We have been playing here (Brisbane) but no good has resulted from it. Shall be glad to get back to Sydney. Keep up the quality of the 10/- set of boxing gloves, you will get some orders for these.'

Shrewsbury's footballing plans took another twist. 'We shall use every endeavour to bring a New Zealand Rugby team back with us, but this had better be kept a profound secret for the time at least.' He went on to suggest that Mr Sadler should look round England for any Australian or New Zealand footballers, who might be incorporated in the proposed team, so as to again save on the cost of passages to and from England. He hoped to bring the New Zealand football team to England in October since this was a slack time for the shipping companies and 'we could get passages at £35 per man first class.' Returning to the tour of Australia, Shrewsbury comments: 'Newham has decided not to stay out, this won't matter much as I don't think he is very well up in football ... The football tour seems to be going all right, and up to now we have obtained first class terms for the use of grounds, but some difficulty may arise if the players require a large share of the takings.'

Back in Sydney after the Queensland tour, the cricketers prepared for the second match against New South Wales with two days of net practice. Good bowling by Johnny Briggs allied to quite exceptional fielding removed the colony for 149. The tourists were 53 for 2 at the close of the first day with Shrewsbury 21 not out and the Notts batsman saw the total to three figures before he was dismissed for 48. The tail end, notably Aubrey Smith, hit out to provide a commanding lead and on the third day victory was obtained by ten wickets. This was a great win, since New South Wales had not only beaten the side in the first game, but also beaten the rival English side. There was a decent crowd – about 10,000 on the second day (Saturday) but poor attendances on the other days. After the game Shrewsbury wrote to Shaw: 'The news re Cricket Tour is not good, in fact as far as I can see at present, without something turns up better than has been the case up to now, it will take us all our time to make it pay. We received for our first match at Sydney (v NSW, Nov 11 and 12) £417 5s 2d and for our second, just finished, (v NSW, Dec 9, 10, 12) I think we will come about the same sum. Then you know what a lot of expenses there are to pay out of this – luncheons, bill posting, adverts etc. Our second match was all that could be desired, the weather being beautiful. NSW went in on a perfect wicket.' Shrewsbury then continues with a description of the match and follows with: 'When the MCC (Vernon's) team was playing at Sydney, they took at the gates before 12.30, the sum of £90 and they certainly would have had an attendance of 12 to 15 thousand if rain had not come on – as it was they took £600 away and had big gates for all the days. People here think they are all amateurs – Gentlemen of England – and that is the reason they get patronage. In our next match I have told Sheridan (the NSW agent for Shrewsbury's team) to advertise our side as 'Gentlemen of England', same as the MCC do ... You will ask why the MCC Team have been allowed to play at Sydney at all. The truth is the Trustees (of the Sydney Ground) have had their hands forced and they are not quite so powerful as they imagined they were. Sheridan told Jim (Lillywhite) that the Manager of the bank where McDonnell, Ferris and Turner are engaged, said that if the MCC Team was not allowed the ground at Sydney for a second match, none of the above players should be allowed to take part in any further matches against us. So the Trustees had to give way again. At the same time it is no doubt doing us a lot of harm and we intend to make an application for the use of the ground free of all costs.'

Returning to the proposed football tour to Australia, Shaw had suggested that some soccer matches be arranged, but Shrewsbury discovered that soccer was not played seriously in Australia. Trouble however was brewing from another quarter. The English Rugby Union was now informed of Shrewsbury's plans and immediately came out in opposition on the grounds that the players were being paid and this infringed the strict amateur status of Rugby Union footballers. Shrewsbury left Shaw to argue this one out.

Shrewsbury's cricketers left Sydney by train for Melbourne. One of the carriages caught fire near Goulburn, which delayed the arrival in the Victorian capital, but the game against the colony began on time. For some unexplained reason Victoria fielded only four of their first eleven in the team which met Shrewsbury's side. Shrewsbury immediately assumed this to be a nasty trick on the part of the Melbourne Club, who were merely going through the motions of giving the rival Shrewsbury team a match at Melbourne. The game was a complete farce, Victoria were dismissed for 62, then the Englishmen replied with 624. Shrewsbury took the opportunity to score 232. On the opening day he reached 86 not out, on the second day he increased his score to 221 not out and was finally dismissed when the score reached 525 for 6. It was the first time an Englishman had hit a double century in Australian first-class cricket. He batted about 7½ hours in all, without making a single mistake until the end. Sadly very few spectators watched the proceedings – in fact more people were present at the following up-country odds match at Ballarat, which gave the tourists another easy victory.

The Sydney-based players retaliated on Shrewsbury's behalf against the shabby treatment meted out to Shrewsbury in Melbourne by refusing to play for Combined Australia (so-called) against Vernon's Team in Melbourne. The game took place immediately following Shrewsbury's match at the same venue and with the same one-sided result. Vernon's Team thrashed 'Australia' by an innings, but the match being played over the New Year holiday the attendance was better than for Shrewsbury's Team.

The mining town of Bendigo was the venue for Shrewsbury's Team over the New Year, but owing to an attack of neuralgia, Shrewsbury remained in Melbourne. Opposition to the football tour now came from the Victorian Football Association, who passed a resolution agreeing not to support the venture. Shrewsbury however pressed ahead. 'Turning to Football matters again,' he wrote to Shaw, 'you would have to get a nice outfit especially made for the team. Something that would be good material and yet take them by storm out here. You could also have a monogram worked on the front of it. The players will have to take a lot of exercise on board ship, or they will be too stout to play for some time when they arrive. They could use the football on board ship for the little kicks from one to another, which is practised to a great extent in the Victorian game, as the players are not allowed to use their hands to throw it to another player.'

The Victorian Football Association considered the matter of the football tour a second time and again refused to support it, though only by thirteen votes against ten. In England the Rugby Union held a meeting and also voted against it on the grounds that it encouraged professionalism. Shrewsbury's reaction was that if the Rugby Union could persuade the players to tour for nothing, he would be delighted, since it would increase his profit. Shrewsbury had approached Stoddart about staying in Australia to play football and the Middlesex batsman stated he would only stay if the Rugby footballer,

Jeffrey – his team-mate at Blackheath – came out. Shaw was given the job of persuading Jeffrey to tour.

The cricket tour continued to go downhill – the matches in Victoria had been a disaster. Shrewsbury noted: 'Am sorry to say we are doing very badly in our cricket and if they don't alter very much we are certain to be money out of pocket.' Other financial transactions looked bleak. Shaw had purchased £500 worth of gold shares in a Ballarat mine on his previous visit and asked Shrewsbury to check on his investment. 'I didn't much like the look of Moss (the broker) when I saw him in Sydney and when I told him he must send your scrip to Messrs Stoddart and Binne, he inquired very pointedly whether I had power of attorney to act for you ... I may find it necessary to sharpen him up when we return to Sydney.'

The cricket team left Victoria by train bound for Sydney, but on the way stopped at the fashionable resort of Bowral, some 80 miles from Sydney itself. An odds game here was won by an innings and the team then went on to Sydney for the third and deciding match with New South Wales. On a rain-affected pitch Charley Turner routed the tourists, his analyses being 8 for 19 and 8 for 26 – he bowled unchanged through both innings. Shrewsbury, who had been convincingly baffled by Turner on the 1886/7 tour, was the only English batsman to master him in this present game, scoring 56 in the second innings out of 129 all out. Shrewsbury wrote home: 'We have lost our third match against NSW. It would have to be something wonderful, if it had been otherwise. They batted on good wickets, we had two bad ones. You never saw such damned bad luck in your life – we had 250 odd to get (to win) and should easily have got them, but the rain came sufficient to make the wickets sticky. I never saw anything like it in my life, we must have several men in the team, who have committed murder. We can beat them on anything like a decent wicket 19 times out of twenty. The financial part of the tour has not improved.'

Whilst in Sydney, Shrewsbury continued his rounds of the sports shops. Going to see Mr Killick he found more blunders by the manager of Shaw and Shrewsbury's business in

Nottingham: 'Mr Killick is an honourable man, but he is thoroughly disgusted with the manner in which our business with him has been conducted, being entirely wrong in every direction. I can tell you candidly I have been ashamed calling upon him and having to so frequently apologise for the numerous errors.' Among these errors was an invoice demanding £82 6s 6d, which ought to have read £6 17s 3d, and the supplying of four dozen bats, when only two dozen were ordered.

As if he did not have enough financial muddles to untangle, Shrewsbury had promised his old school friend, Will Scotton, that he would retrieve a debt of £40, which a firm owed Scotton from the sale of bats during the previous tour. Shrewsbury went to some trouble to attempt to obtain the £40, only to discover that the money had been sent to England and there was little doubt that Scotton was aware of the fact and, through Shrewsbury, was trying to cheat the Australian firm. Shrewsbury wrote to Shaw asking him to have a sharp word with Scotton. The latter's reaction was to lend all his cricket trophies to the rival firm of Gunn and Moore for a window display. Shrewsbury commented: 'It is just the kind of thing he would only be too glad of the opportunity to do.' The school chums were obviously no longer friends.

Two up-country games were played and the team then came back to Sydney for a match against Combined Australia. The four-day game provided Shrewsbury's team with a five-wicket win, due mainly to the bowling of Lohmann who took twelve wickets. Several of the best Victorian players did not appear. The next match, also at Sydney, was supposed to be the greatest ever played, in that the two English touring teams temporarily sank their differences, selected a combined eleven and played Australia. The leading Victorian players, as in the previous fixture, refused to take part, ruining this arrangement. In a low-scoring game Australia were easily beaten. Shrewsbury hit the best score of the match. The report noted: 'Shrewsbury's innings was the salvation of his side' – he scored 44 out of 113 all out. Yet another major fixture for Shrewsbury's team in Sydney was against the

Australian team selected to tour England in 1888. Once more
the Englishmen were victorious and again Shrewsbury made
the highest score of the match. He made 51, when he was
bowled 'by Turner with a terrible breakneck'. The game was
finished in two days and hardly 2,000 attended.

The final first-class match was a return against the 1888
Australians, also staged in Sydney. Like so many on the tour
it was dominated by Shrewsbury, who hit another double
century. After the first innings of each side had been played
the match was even, but with Shrewsbury hitting 206 and
the total reaching 402, the visitors won by 158 runs.

The first-class averages for the tour simply demonstrate
Shrewsbury's overwhelming superiority. He hit 766 runs,
average 58·92 – the next batsman, Brann, hit 158 and averaged 26·33. The team was most successful, Lohmann and
Briggs being the most effective bowlers, but financially the
visit was quite depressing – it says much for Shrewsbury's
ability that he could score runs, whilst his mind was trying
to grapple with the pecuniary aspects of the tour and by
organising the football tours to save his own money.

Back in Nottingham, Shaw was not proving very apt in the
running of the shop and factory. For some reason Shaw did
not trust Sadler, the shop manager, and engaged Bates, the
former manager of Richard Daft's shop, to supervise Sadler.
This of course upset Sadler, though luckily he did not resign.
Shrewsbury didn't trust Bates, or the factory manager, Trimmings, but there was little he could do whilst he was in
Australia. In the correspondence between Shaw and Shrewsbury there are at this time ominous pointers that the management of the business was not soundly based, but it was to
be some time before any concrete evidence appeared.

After the match against the 1888 Australians, the team
prepared to leave for a short programme of matches in New
Zealand. Shrewsbury sends his final letter from the Oxford
Hotel, Sydney to Shaw:

'Dear Alfred, Your letter dated Feb 2/88 duly to hand. I
note what you say re sending some cash home and will do
so, as soon as we possibly can. I have had to cash that draft,

I brought over here, for £400 and we have run so very short that Mr Faithful, the solicitor, has been kind enough to be bound for us at the Bank for £600 or £700. I can tell you we have been pretty hard pressed, having had to pay £800 to £1,000 a/c to the New Zealand Shipping Co for the team coming out and home. We expect that as soon as they arrive, we shall commence picking up some money and by all accounts the Football team is bound to be a big success. Of course that very much depends whether you have sent out first class players. I expected, when they left England for New Zealand, the names would be cabled out, but such has not been done. It is very necessary they should beat the NZ men, who, I am told, are A.1. We are sure to lose a lot of money by the cricket venture, but hope to get it back at football. I will write you more particulars of this when we arrive in NZ, for which colony we start on Saturday next – you will be pleased to hear (*though this must be kept a profound secret*) that the trustees gave us a rebate of £150 and I think we shall obtain the ground (i.e. Sydney) pretty cheap for football. We received your wire about a week back saying Smith (C. Aubrey Smith) must come home and since then he has had another from his father, asking him to do so on account of his mother's illness. I expect this is all a sham and is only a pretence to get him back home, as Alcock and Betts (presumably C. W. Alcock and M. P. Betts) have, I think, been trying to instil into his father's mind that he will be regarded as a professional, should he stay out. Brann also agreed to stay, but now Smith is going home, he says he will go also. I am heartily glad they are both going, as I am sick and tired of the way they have been humbugging us for some time. Smith has thought nothing of saying one day he would stay and in a week after would come as cool as possible and tell you he wouldn't be able to. Brann said at first his leg would not stand the strain, but when Smith said he would stay, the leg soon got better and he agreed to stay with Smith. I tell you candidly I am pleased they are going home and think it will be £600 in our pockets by them doing so. We were having to pay them £200 each in expenses. The only thing we are afraid of just now is that should Stoddart hear they are not staying, he will want to go home as well. However he don't know about this yet and we sent him a cheque for £50 a few days since, which should bind him. He wrote to us to say he had a friend in Melbourne, who was just about sailing for home, but if we would pay his travelling expenses he would stay out and play football with us – his name's R. C. Tryston and am told by Stoddart he is a very good player. We should not have to pay his passage home – so you see we shall manage without Smith and Brann and in the meantime shall look about us to get another good player who may be out here and able to play the Victorian game. We received your cable the other day saying the team had left direct for NZ. Stoddart was looking at a match in Melbourne Saturday last and he says an English Rugby player would not have the slightest difficulty in picking the Victorian game up. I wish you had asked Tinsley Lindsay (Notts cricketer, Cambridge Rugby and soccer blue) to come out, a few first class Association players would have been very serviceable for the Victorian game. Should imagine he would have come. I think I said in my last letter we were paying 80 gns for the round trip. If you have arranged with the London Office for £81, we must get the balance back. The attendance during our last match (v 1888 Australians in Sydney) was a failure, in fact it scarcely pays expenses playing here even in big matches.'

In Victoria, the rival English Team fared even worse during their last match, very few spectators witnessing the game, the whole interest of which centred on the performance of Walter Read, since a great newspaper contest had built up as to whether Read was a better batsman than Shrewsbury. Their averages were followed closely. Shrewsbury had hit a double century in his final innings and Read needed the same to keep up. He scored 24 and 142 not out and the final first-class averages for the two ended with Shrewsbury 58·92 and Read 55·45. In all matches each batsman averaged 37.

Whilst Vernon's Team sailed for home, Shrewsbury and his men, except for Docker, who stayed in Australia, sailed aboard the SS *Hantoro* for Wellington. With heavy seas for most of the five-day voyage, the cricketers had a gruelling time. The weather delayed the arrival of the team, so that the first match, against Wellington, had to start a day late. The players settled in at the Post Office Hotel, Wellington, and Shrewsbury began his rounds of the town's sports outfitters. The team moved on to Christchurch, where the two final matches of the tour were played, both being odds matches against eighteen of Canterbury and both drawn. Shrewsbury made little money from the three New Zealand games and suspected that the gatekeepers were swindling him – the crowds did not seem to match the receipts. With no money left, Shrewsbury had to write home telling Shaw how much they owed each cricketer – Newham £146 16s 3d; Brann £189 17s 6d; Lohmann £80; Read £100; Briggs £60; Pilling £55; Preston £45; Pougher £75; Ulyett £130 less £57 4s 2d. He was still optimistic however, continuing: 'As we obtain cash for footballing we shall cable you some over to pay the above sums with, but may not send sufficient all at once to cover the amounts. In that case you must make Newham and Brann wait until the others are paid. Ulyett told Jim (Lillywhite) he was not particular to a month or two; at the same time I should prefer to pay them as soon as possible. Newham and Brann won't tell anyone they are not paid, you can rely on that.' (Newham and Brann were, of course, the so-called amateurs.)

While awaiting in New Zealand the arrival of the foot-ballers – the cricketers left Port Lyttelton aboard the SS *Coptic* on 31 March – Shrewsbury continued his sales campaign, sending vast details on shops and their potential retail goods back to England. He had not forgotten however that the cricket season would soon be starting in England: 'You must send me accounts of the cricket in England this summer. The Australians are sure to be badly beaten, in fact any good team will easily lick them on a good wicket. It is a farce them playing England.' Shrewsbury was correct in his assessment, the side's batting being very suspect and the 1888 Australians were very dependent on their two leading bowlers, Turner and Ferris.

The football team had sailed from Gravesend aboard the SS *Kaikoura* on 8 March. Although not thoroughly representative of English Rugby football, they were a strong side and consisted of: J. T. Haslam (Yorkshire and Batley), A. Paul (Lancashire and Swinton) backs; H. C. Speakman (Cheshire and Runcorn), Dr H. Brooks (Durham and Edinburgh University), J. Anderton (Lancashire and Salford) three-quarter backs; W. Bumby (Lancashire and Swinton), J. Nolan (Rochdale Hornets), W. Burnett (Roxburgh and Hawick) half-backs; C. Mathers (Yorkshire and Bramley), S. Williams (Lancashire and Salford), T. Banks (Lancashire and Swinton), R. L. Seddon (Lancashire and Swinton), H. Eagles (Lancashire and Swinton), A. J. Stuart (Yorkshire and Dewsbury), W. H. Thomas (Cambridge University and Wales), J. P. Clowes (Yorkshire and Halifax), T. Kent (Lancashire and Salford), A. P. Penketh (Douglas, Isle of Man), R. Burnett (Roxburgh and Hawick), A. J. Laing (Roxburgh and Hawick) forwards. Dr J. Smith, the Scottish soccer international, travelled as umpire.

The captain of the team was R. L. Seddon. In a tragic accident he was drowned whilst sculling on the river Hunter at Maitland and A. E. Stoddart took over as captain for the remainder of the tour. They played a total of 53 matches, 19 of which were in New Zealand.

Shrewsbury's financial situation did not improve. On 24 April, the day after the football team landed, he wrote from the Grand Hotel, Dunedin: 'We will send you some cash as soon as possible. You must know that it has taken us all our time to keep this scheme going. As we have been terribly short of funds, we have to leave bills unsettled at our hotel and also could not pay the commission on the cricket ground at Christchurch for use of the cricket team there. I can tell you we have had to act with great caution and diplomacy, but think all will be well now if we can only have fine weather for the first few matches.'

Shaw was also beginning to worry. He suggested that they should float the firm on the stock market and estimated it to be worth £20,000. Shaw looked into the possibility of bringing the football team back via the United States, playing matches as they went, but this, remembering the cricket disaster of 1881/2, was not an idea Shrewsbury was keen to consider, especially as the travelling would cost an extra £500. There were schemes afoot to bring a Maori Rugby team to England for 1888/9 and Shrewsbury therefore abandoned his plan to recruit a New Zealand Rugby team.

The business of the Melbourne-sponsored English team advertising themselves as 'Gentlemen of England' still grated, and when Shrewsbury spotted a paragraph in a Melbourne paper, he wrote home to Shaw: 'I enclose you a cutting re Walter Read being paid £1,000 for coming out here and also wanting more than the Melbourne Club would allow him for expenses. I remember about a fortnight or three weeks before leaving home, Vernon (the captain) wrote to the *Sporting Life* or *Sportsman* denying that Read would be paid anything but his bare expenses. He must have known when he was doing this, that he was telling a deliberate lie. Try and get someone to write to the papers regarding Mr Vernon's letter and enquire whether Read was paid this amount. How (was it that) Read did not write to the papers himself instead of getting Vernon to do it for him. He wants showing up.'

The football matches began in the last week of April: 'We played our first match last Saturday amidst great excitement, in fact all over NZ great interest is being exhibited. After the first half, we thought we might lose, as Otago had obtained a goal and our side one try. In the second half however we had a little wind in our favour and had the game pretty much our own way. Cricketers never had half the reception as the footballers are having, being driven in drags, taken boating, dancing, dinner parties, free entrance to rinks, in fact everything is being done for their enjoyment. Some who had an opportunity of coming will bite their finger nails off when they hear this – I know nothing of this kind has ever been done with cricket teams. The papers said 10,000 people were present, but returns show only 6,000. I don't know, but there certainly to me appeared to be 8,000.'

Shrewsbury seemed to accept the appointment by Shaw of Bates as manager of the Nottingham shop: 'I hope Bates will

turn out well, as if he is a valuable man, he can do us good.
Sadler told me before I engaged him that Daft had said he
would get rid of Bates very soon. If he is a really good man,
Daft has acted simple in losing him.' Whilst it was apparent
that Daft had little business sense, the reason for the releasing
of Bates may well have been that H. B. Daft, Richard's son
and one of the most promising all-round sportsmen of his
generation, being an international soccer player as well as a
county cricketer, had joined his father's business as a partner.
In 1888 Daft's Nottingham shop was described as 'The largest
Athletic Emporium in the World'.

The footballers had drawn their game in Wellington and
Shrewsbury comments, 'The second game was played in a
much fairer spirit than the first one, though unfortunately
one of the Wairarapa players had his leg broken – we had
four of our men injured in the first match here and should
require 50 men if each game was played as roughly as the
Saturday match. The papers give so one-sided an account,
that none of us are sending any home.'

The first financial calculations for the football tour were
that the overall cost would be about £6,000. ('Of course,'
Shrewsbury cautions Shaw, 'we tell everyone it will cost
£8,000 or £9,000 and you may tell them even more.')

The football team met its first defeat at the hands of Tar-
anaki in New Plymouth: 'though we actually won, getting
two tries which the referee disallowed. He not only disallowed
the tries, but refused to take off the time spent in discussing
the matter, which was about 12 minutes. There were four
brothers playing in the match, two being players, one umpire
and one referee. We were not likely to win with this combination against us.' After their relative success, the team sailed
to Sydney to play Rugby against teams in New South Wales.
Shrewsbury still thought he was being diddled by the gate-
men – in the first Sydney match, he estimated the crowd at
12,000, but the official figures showed only 7,000.

From New South Wales to Victoria, where Shrewsbury
hoped to make money. The transition from Rugby football to
Victorian Rules however was not quite the simple process he

had imagined. 'I can play better than some of our players,' he commented, 'who don't shape at all and never will. The elder Burnett and Anderton are very good, whilst Stoddart and a few others are also likely to make good men at it. We play a big match tomorrow with a certain licking before us.'

By the time the side arrived in South Australia in July, the business was turning quite sour: 'Since we arrived in Victoria we have done very badly indeed, all on account of our players not being able to play the game. Contrary to my expectations, they don't improve half as much as I expected and the sooner we are away from the game and at the Rugby the better ... So you will see the tour is not likely to turn out the good thing we expected after all, in fact, without something very unexpected and lucky turning up, we shall only just come out about straight at the finish.'

After playing in Australia it was arranged that the team sail back to New Zealand for a second series of matches before returning home. Shrewsbury however was having difficulty arranging these final matches on satisfactory terms, 'simply through our players not taking care of themselves – too much whisky and women.'

Back home, the factory manager, Trimmings, asked Shaw for an increase in his wages and Shaw consulted Shrewsbury, who answered: 'Both Trimmings and Clarke (another employee) had their salaries raised when I was at home and the former's was conditional on him taking the management of the shop, which I afterwards found he was not able to. He never asked for an increase, but placing him in a position, as I thought, of greater responsibility, it was necessary to raise his screw at the same time. As you say, they had better wait until I come home, then we can discuss the matter fully. No doubt they have both set their heads together in this respect. My opinion about Trimmings, since I overheard what he said to Clarke after I had given him a rise, is that you will have to keep a very sharp look out after him. He requires a lot of watching and either you or myself should always be in the workshop. He is clever with his tongue, but not the slightest notice should be taken of this. My advice is, don't give him a

chance of doing wrong, for fear he might take it – your son
Jack [Shaw's son was employed in the factory making bats]
is a great check and will be more so as he grows older and is
better able to understand what is right and wrong. Richardson (the shop manager in 1886) began with borrowing
money and in my opinion it is a very bad sign. You will, I
am afraid, have great difficulty in getting your £10 back, also
Scotton's £5. Am afraid Trimmings will also corrupt Clarke
and Bates, if you are not careful. It is very easy for him to
say his department is paying (which I should take with great
reserve) but we must have this verified to our own satisfac-
tion.'

There was little improvement in the football tour finances,
but the success of the Shaw and Shrewsbury patent bat was
worrying other manufacturers. The bat was a double-spliced
spring handle bat, which was a great improvement on other
bats since it went a long way to removing any sting or jar-
ring. George Frowd of the London sports firm of Jas Lillywhite,
Frowd and Co. was threatening to take Shaw and Shrewsbury
to court because he claimed the Nottingham firm had infringed his patent bat. Shrewsbury gave Shaw the following
advice: 'I should fight Frowd re patent bat, if you are advised
there is any chance of winning ... He is a grabbing sort of
fellow and wouldn't let anyone live but himself.' The character of Trimmings cropped up again, Shrewsbury wondered
whether the wages Trimmings drew for the workers in the
factory all went into the right pockets. The question of factory
stock-taking arose and Shrewsbury noted: 'Look what a scope
Trimmings has with the tennis gut, which is very expensive.
As regards the quantity of gut required for one bat or quantity
of bats, the people you buy the gut off would be only too glad
to give you all the information you require. You would then
know whether Trimmings used all the gut he received by the
bats he turns out.'

Another, lesser, problem cropped up: 'I was thinking about
our telephone at the shop the other day and would advise
you, unless the price was reduced to about one quarter, not
to renew it. I told Sadler when I was at home not to renew

it, but I think he made a mull of it in some way and did exactly what I told him not to do. Blackburn, whom we leased the factory from, said he could put us in a telephone for about £10 or £15 and it would be our own and nothing further to pay. Would see to this. These telephone people will take about a quarter of what they first ask. Would rather not have a telephone than pay what we have been doing for it.'

The final matches in New Zealand did not produce much profit – the local clubs took advantage of Shrewsbury's weak position and demanded 40 per cent of the gate, as against the 25 per cent they received in the early matches. Shrewsbury had to accept the situation. Shaw wrote to complain that the cricketers had still not been paid and Shrewsbury managed to cable him £350 – about half the required sum. Money was also needed urgently for willow for next season's bats. Shrewsbury reckoned to require enough to make about four to five thousand bats.

The ideas of bringing a New Zealand team to England and taking the English team to America in the hope of salvaging something from the financial ruins had fallen flat. Shaw even suggested staging a Victorian Rules football match in England, but this was quickly cast aside when it was discovered that the only possible opponents were Australians resident at Edinburgh University – not a contest to draw the British public!

So Shrewsbury's long absence from Nottingham was almost at an end. The cricket tour had lost £2,400 and the football tour a further £800. What made matters much worse was the inability of the third partner in these enterprises, Jim Lillywhite, to shoulder any of this debt. Shrewsbury therefore had to produce £1,600 to clear the debts instead of £1,070.

8 Ups and Downs Back in England

It was not until December 1888 that Arthur Shrewsbury landed back in England, having been absent for about fifteen months. His immediate engagement was at the Town Hall in Nottingham, where a select gathering presided over by the Mayor wished to present the cricketer with an illuminated address and a purse containing seventy-two sovereigns, the result of a collection, limited to five shillings per person, in recognition of his record breaking season of 1887. Shrewsbury was much embarrassed by the ceremony being held in the Town Hall, because protocol meant that he would have to deliver a speech of thanks bareheaded. As a young man he had become bald and was exceedingly sensitive regarding this, so much so that even in the pavilion dressing room he contrived to change and to switch from cricket cap to ordinary headgear without revealing his baldness. It is said that he attempted to arrange for the presentation of the address to be made in the Trent Bridge pavilion, but this he failed to do. The original notes he wrote for his speech for thanks are still preserved and read as follows:

'I should like in the first place to express to you gentlemen who have contributed to this testimonial my warmest and most grateful thanks. It is always gratifying to a cricketer to know, whether by a word of encouragement or in any other manner, that his efforts on the cricket field have been observed. It is scarcely necessary to point out to you gentlemen that it has always been my aim whilst playing cricket to do the utmost for my side, never wishing to take an unfair or undue advantage and at the same time, to concede none.

'If you will allow me I should like to state my reasons for

staying on the other side of the globe during the last cricket season in England. It has been said by some few unkind and uncharitable individuals, that I ought to have placed everything else on one side so as to have been at home to have assisted my county. I was engaged in what I may term a perfectly legitimate business transaction, involving the outlay of some thousands of pounds. Twelve months previously I had agreed with Mr Lillywhite, one of the partners, that, should a tour take place, I would stay out and assist in the management. It would have been worse than mean, it would have been dishonest to have shirked my responsibility and left him to manage as best he could. I was on the spot and represented two-thirds of the outlay. You gentlemen, who have never been engaged in anything of the kind, can have no adequate idea of the amount of labour, anxiety and diplomacy required if you are to bring matters to a successful termination.

'Travelling about Australia and New Zealand is not all pleasure. Twenty to thirty hours at a stretch in a railway carriage slowly creeping along with bad sleeping and refreshment accommodation is an experience not to be desired. The frequent short journey along the coast of New Zealand, sick and ill the whole time, is equally unpleasant, and not at all to my taste. Playing cricket would have been a real pleasure compared to this, but I suppose we have all certain duties we owe to ourselves and which we are not entitled to ignore.

'However let us hope in the cricket season that is fast drawing near, Notts will show more of her true form than she did last season. The position she occupied then certainly cannot be taken as indicating her real merit, or of what we are capable of doing. We can only hope to retrieve ourselves, not only by the strength of the team, but what is equally important, the most cordial good feeling existing between the executive and the players.

'I only hope, gentlemen, it may be my good fortune to retain the respect and esteem of my many friends in Nottingham and elsewhere for many years to come.

'I wish to thank His Worship the Mayor for presiding over

this meeting and Lord Belper for marking the occasion by his presence here today. Also Mr Cressey, Mr Royle and other gentlemen who have worked so indefatigably during my absence. Your Worship, Lord Belper, gentlemen, I beg with every sincerity to thank you.'

In 1888 summer had been a dismally wet one in England, but the lack of sunshine had not affected Surrey's triumphant progress; having taken the Championship title away from Notts in 1887, the southern county won twelve of its fourteen first-class county matches, though curiously it was beaten twice by the Australians, of whom Shrewsbury had such a low estimation. In contrast Notts could do no more than struggle from one disaster to another. Without Shrewsbury's inspiration the batting seemed to fall apart. In the fourteen county matches, not a single individual hundred was scored. Scotton's impregnable defence failed utterly – he averaged 14 with the bat. Gunn did little until the final matches and Barnes scarcely averaged 20. Almost the only man to enhance his reputation was Henry Richardson from Bulwell. Unlike Surrey, Notts beat the Australians twice, due to Attewell's bowling, which had been so useful to Vernon's team in Australia. The team taken to Australia by Shrewsbury met the 1888 Australians twice in England in September – at Leeds and at Old Trafford – and even without the Notts batsman won both games with ease. Surrey therefore retained the Championship title, whilst Notts languished near the foot of the table, a position they had only suffered before in 1881 during the strike.

'Notts, with the champion professional cricketer once more at home, ought to make a good fight to recover their lost position amongst the Counties', ran the opening sentence of the magazine *Cricket* in its preview of Notts for 1889. There was no need to mention Shrewsbury by name.

The county was now under new leadership, with the easy-going Sherwin replaced by the more serious-minded amateur, J. A. Dixon. Although he had appeared for Notts on and off since 1882, he was better known as a soccer player, having been capped by England at outside left. The fixtures

opened with the Sussex match at Trent Bridge. Dixon won
the toss and accompanied by Shrewsbury began the innings.
The new captain was soon dismissed, but Shrewsbury, 'making runs far faster than has been his wont, was seen to the
greatest advantage, playing all the bowling with great freedom and confidence.' His 104 came in 180 minutes. The
match was won early on the third day by an innings.

This initial success seemed to boost the team's confidence
and the next five first-class inter-county matches – against
Middlesex, Surrey, Lancashire, the return with Sussex, and
Kent – were all innings victories. Shrewsbury played little
part in this astonishing run, being absent injured from two
games and scoring only one half-century in the others.
William Gunn scored most runs, but the bowling was very
much a team effort. There was a close-fought match at Bramall Lane, where a good all-round performance by Bobby
Peel broke the Notts sequence of innings wins, but victory
was obtained by 36 runs. Gloucestershire were beaten by an
innings, and then came the match of the season – the August
Bank Holiday game with Surrey.

The Bank Holiday Monday was a miserable day, but
20,863 spectators actually paid admission to watch Surrey
bat between heavy showers. Even on Tuesday, with more
rain, over 16,000 attended, but the great day was the final
one. Lockwood, the colt Notts had rejected two seasons earlier, played a fine innings and allowed Surrey to make a
declaration – this was the first season the law allowing declarations had been in force. The wicket was very difficult,
drying under a hot sun, and Notts required 219 in 180 minutes. They could only play for a draw. Harry Daft opened
with Shrewsbury, but soon went. Then Gunn was removed
for a single. Billy Barnes joined Arthur and by careful batting
the pair pushed the total to 63. Both were then dismissed and
the remainder of the side, against the tricky bowling of Lohmann, fell like a house of cards, no one reaching double
figures. The crowd of about 13,000 invaded the pitch and
the cheering was prolonged.

The wet weather followed Notts back to Trent Bridge. The

game with Middlesex was drawn due to rain. On the Clifton
College ground a rain-affected pitch produced some interesting cricket. W. G. Grace won the toss and decided to bat, only
to see Gloucestershire dismissed for 105. Notts however could
manage just 87, of which Shrewsbury made 23, then in still
difficult conditions Gloucester fell for 60, leaving Notts 79 to
make in the final innings. Wilfred Flowers was chosen to
open with Shrewsbury, and quite remarkably for such a low
scoring game, the pair hit off the runs without being
separated, though Gloucester did not help their cause by giving each batsman one chance. On the same day Lancashire
surprised everyone by defeating Surrey at the Oval and these
two results left the race for the Championship title very interesting – Notts, Surrey or Lancashire being in a position to
take the crown.

Rain forced draws in both the matches involving Notts and
Surrey on the following days, but Lancashire beat Kent by an
innings. In the next series of matches, Notts met Lancashire
in a washed-out draw: 'probably no match which had been
anticipated with widespread interest, was so completely
ruined by bad weather'. However Surrey took advantage by
beating Kent. This left just two fixtures which would decide
the Championship, Kent v Notts at Beckenham and Surrey v
Yorkshire at the Oval. The latter was played first and Surrey
won a tremendous tussle by two wickets. Notts therefore travelled to Beckenham knowing that they had to beat Kent, to
secure the honours.

The Beckenham wicket had a reputation for helping the
bowlers and a heavy dew on the first morning made Dixon
think twice before deciding to bat. By lunch Notts had
reached 61 for the loss of Dixon, Shrewsbury and Barnes.
The rest of the batsmen only just managed to double the
score. Kent were 44 for 1 at stumps. On the second morning
Kent collapsed and Notts gained a first innings lead of 16,
and at lunch Notts were 24 for 2, thus increasing their lead
to 40. After the interval an incredible change came over the
game, Notts losing eight wickets for 11 runs, thus leaving
Kent needing only 52 to win. Dick Attewell made a great

effort to pull the game round – Kent slumped to 25 for 6. Fatally Sherwin missed a chance of running out Barton, and he with George Hearne nudged Kent to victory, thus depriving Notts of the outright title. Attewell's second innings analysis was 25–21–7–4. Nottinghamshire therefore shared the Championship with both Surrey and Lancashire, a state of affairs which prompted much newspaper discussion. The system of deciding the title – one point for a win and half for a draw – had been in vogue only two years and was in any case only a device invented by the newspapers and not sanctioned by either the first-class counties themselves or by the MCC. The printer who issued the scorecards at Trent Bridge firmly claimed the title for Nottinghamshire alone, under the old system of least matches lost – Notts lost two, while Surrey and Lancashire lost three each – but it seems C.H. Richards was a voice on his own and Wisden's editor, with the other cricket reporters, claimed a triple tie.

Suffering two injuries, Shrewsbury played through the season with some disadvantage, but the general wet summer ended with Arthur being second to Gunn in the first-class averages as a whole, but only by the smallest margin – Gunn 37·68, Shrewsbury 37·28. Only nine cricketers managed a batting average above 30 in 1889. The combination of his injuries and his business commitments meant that Shrewsbury played in only one first-class fixture outside the county programme – the Gentlemen v Players game at the Oval, where he captained the latter to a nine-wicket victory and scored 57 in his only innings. Alfred Shaw was now almost entirely occupied by his engagement with Lord Sheffield in Sussex and the affairs of Shaw and Shrewsbury were very much in the hands of Shrewsbury. The losses made on the two tours to Australia meant that money had to be borrowed from the bank to buy in stock, and in order to economise Shrewsbury took some drastic measures. He closed both the retail shop in Carrington Street and the factory in Waterway Street and reopened the business under a single roof at 6 Queen's Bridge Road.

The new premises had a road frontage of some 90 feet and

the plot extended back 120 feet, the main workshop being 25
feet wide and 60 feet in length. Part of it was two-storey,
with the manufacture of bats being on the ground floor and
of pads and leather goods on the first floor. There was also a
retail shop on the road frontage, but the major part of the
business was in the wholesale trade. Financial considerations
obviously demanded this change, but in retrospect it handed
over some of the existing retail business to the rival Gunn
and Moore firm, whose shop was now in Carrington Street.
Queen's Bridge Road joined Arkwright Street at the Queen's
Hotel and therefore Shrewsbury could look out from his bedroom window to his firm across the road.

Shrewsbury's first-class cricket for 1890 began in the un-
usual setting of Sheffield Park, Lord Sheffield's private ground,
some fifteen miles north of Brighton. Shrewsbury was part of
an England side opposing the 1890 Australians for their first
match. The Australians made 190 for 8 on the first day, rain
totally washed out the second, and England, caught on a
sticky wicket, were dismissed for 27 and 130 on the third
day, with Turner and Ferris being unplayable. Shrewsbury
achieved nothing, but he soon made amends. With William
Gunn he created a new world record in the very next match
– Notts v Sussex at Trent Bridge. The two distinguished batsmen added 398 for the second wicket. On the first day, Dixon,
who opened with Shrewsbury, was dismissed with the total
at 26, and by the close the scoreboard showed 341 for 1,
Shrewsbury 164 and Gunn 152. The partnership was broken
when Gunn was caught for 196. This mishap did not affect
his colleague. The report of the game goes on: 'Shrewsbury
continued to play steady, careful and scientific cricket until
he had amassed the huge score of 267, after batting altogether eight hours and fifty minutes, and with the exception
of one chance when he had made 74, there was no flaw in
his batting.' Curiously 267 just equalled his previous highest
innings. The partnership was to remain a County Championship second wicket record for no fewer than 84 years and a
world first-class record for any wicket for nine years. Notts
reached a total of 590 and cruised to an innings victory,

thus beginning the summer in the same manner as its predecessor.

Shrewsbury's innings was made against the relatively weak
Sussex attack, but he took the opportunity at Lord's a few
days later to prove that he could still master the best bowling.
The North opposed the South in a benefit game at Lord's.
Two representative sides were gathered and on a rain-affected
pitch the South were all out for 109. The North struggled
harder and were dismissed for 90. Arthur had opened the
batting and the report comments: 'Shrewsbury's remarkable
performance redeemed the general display of the Northerners
from discredit. He carried his bat through the innings, and at
no time did he seem to be in the least troubled by the bowling,
which puzzled all the other batsmen. His runs were got in his
usual polished style, and without anything like a flaw.' He
made 54 not out, the only double-figure score, and in the
second innings virtually repeated his performance with 34
out of 109 all out. Surrey's George Lohmann was the successful bowler with 11 for 110 in the match. Lohmann, who
played such a part in the success of Surrey at this time, was
forced out of county cricket through ill-health at the age of
31 and died of consumption five years later.

From Lord's Shrewsbury went to Trent Bridge for the Whitsun game with Surrey. Following the battle the previous season, the Nottingham public and indeed cricket fans every-
where regarded the match as of tremendous importance.
About 12,000 attended the first day's play, despite cold
weather. Lohmann had the best bowling figures for the visitors, but Frank Shacklock of Notts bowled even better and
Notts won by 108 runs. Shrewsbury played two useful innings of 41 and 38.

Notts met with a reverse at the hands of Middlesex, but the
four following games were all won at a canter – against Kent,
the return with Sussex, the first game against the Australians
and the Bramall Lane meeting with Yorkshire.

With the season approaching the half-way stage in the
third week of June, Notts were level with Yorkshire at the top
of the Championship table – after the triple tie of 1889, the

counties met and changed the system of awarding points.
The method for 1890 was therefore simply to deduct losses
from wins and ignore draws.

From this point on however Notts went downhill – terrible
fielding, nine catches being dropped in a single afternoon,
allowed Lancashire to force a draw. Shrewsbury's splendid
batting, 117 and 76 not out, could not compensate for the
out-cricket. This allowed Surrey to catch Notts in the table.

A break in the county programme gave Shrewsbury the
chance to captain the Players v Gentlemen both at the Oval
and Lord's. He played four good innings and achieved victory
on the Surrey ground, while rain prevented a finish at Lord's.
Rain also ruined Notts' match with Kent, but the southern
county had the better of what play took place. Surrey slipped
ahead of Notts in the Championship race, but Shrewsbury's
batting was up to form, with an average to 17 July of 76.

A win against Middlesex revived Notts' hopes, but the
county was beaten by another rejected colt – Jack Sharpe of
Ruddington – in the August Bank Holiday game. This fresh
recruit to the Surrey colours took 11 for 89 and Notts lost by
seven wickets. Any lingering thoughts of the title were extin-
guished by another defeat at the hands of the erratic Gloucestershire.

Shrewsbury's batting average was so far above everyone
else in July that whatever happened he was bound to be the
batsman of the year. As it was his average tumbled from 76
to 41 by the season's close, but the next in the list – William
Gunn – averaged only 34. Shrewsbury's lack of success was
not confined to county games. He played without distinction
in both Tests, not that that was remarkable, since every other
batsman failed – the highest team total of the eight played
was only 176. It was a bowler's paradise, Ferris and Turner
having an enjoyable time.

Surrey had more or less sewn up the Championship by
mid-August; Notts ended in fifth place, having won five
matches and lost the same number. It was unfortunate for
Notts that Shrewsbury's lack of form in July and August was
mirrored by Gunn, but of more concern was the failure of

Billy Barnes who could do nothing right all summer. Of the bowlers, the youngster, Richardson, did not progress as hoped and Frank Shacklock, though on occasion effective, was erratic, which left Dick Attewell as the only really reliable man. The Notts Committee must have been slightly annoyed that they had allowed both Lockwood and Sharpe to go to Surrey.

The season over, Shrewsbury concentrated his thoughts on the business, though he still had interests in the family lace firm to consider. His extensive sales drive in Australia and New Zealand proved most lucrative. Shrewsbury appointed Frank Illingworth of Melbourne, who was connected with the East Melbourne Club, as the firm's Australian agent. One or two bad debts surfaced. Patrick McShane, the Australian Test cricketer, had taken some goods on approval. Shrewsbury wrote to Illingworth: 'If your friend would call upon McShane and have a witness there, you might frighten the goods or cash from him – perhaps if the secretary of the club where he is engaged was told of the particulars of the affair, he might bring some pressure to bear upon him.' McShane was later to become mentally unbalanced and confined to an asylum.

Lord Sheffield wrote to Shrewsbury asking his advice concerning a possible tour to Australia in 1891/2 financed by his lordship. Shrewsbury sent some details of the financial aspects of his four tours and was at pains to point out the unbusinesslike behaviour of Jim Lillywhite and the losses of 1887/8. Going to some trouble, Shrewsbury worked out a theoretical income and expenditure account for the proposed tour:

Nottingham
February 27th/91

Estimate of expenses for Cricket Team leaving England about Sep 18th/91, returning May 5th/92, being 21 weeks in the colonies.

	£	s
Passage to and from Australia for 13 men at £100 ea	1300	
Salaries for above at average per man £250	3250	
Journey to London to join ship and one night hotel for 13 men at £2 ea	26	

Return journey rail only from London at per man 30/-	19	10
Stewards fees on board ship, out and home, per man £2	26	
Laundry work for clothing per man per week at 4/-	54	12
Hotel charges for 13 players for 21 weeks at 9/- per day	859	19
Servants at hotels for 21 weeks at per man £3	63	
Railway travelling, say each man per week 30/-	409	10
Sleeping cars for 10 journeys for 13 players at 12/-	78	
Luncheons at 8 big matches, 4 days ea match for 13 men ea 4/-	282	
Band at 8 matches for 1 day ea match (Saturday) at per day £10	80	
Adv. Posters etc for 8 matches at per match £8	64	
Agents for arranging matches and attending to all matters connected with the team	100	
Telegrams, stamps, stationery etc for Agent	20	
	6632	11

Estimated receipts for matches played in Australian season 1891/2

4 Representative Matches at Sydney, average each match £600					2400
4	do	Melbourne,	do	£500	2000
2	do	Adelaide,	do	£300	600
18 Country matches average ea match £100					1800
					£6800

Note: 1886/7 tour of Shaw, Shrewsbury and Lillywhite Cricket Team to the Colonies, twelve representative matches were played (not including Adelaide) at Melbourne and Sydney, and 20 Country Matches, in all 32.

Shrewsbury however cautioned his lordship regarding the inclusion of amateurs in the team: 'I was told when in Australia the expenses of each amateur member of Lord Harris's Team was more than double those of any one of the professionals ... Should Dr W. G. Grace go out, I should imagine, looking at the matter in a purely pecuniary point of view, that his presence would make at the very least £1,500 or £2,000 difference in the takings. It is probable it would exceed this amount. A young generation of cricketers has sprung up since Dr Grace's last visit and many would flock to see him play, who have only read of his great reputation.' (Note: Grace had only toured Australia once before, in 1873/4, under the sponsorship of the Melbourne Club.)

Shrewsbury suggested that Frank Illingworth should act as Lord Sheffield's Australian agent and this was agreed to.

Shrewsbury also wrote to his contacts in New Zealand, notably Mr Mumford in Auckland, to see if the New Zealanders
were interested in any matches against Lord Sheffield's Team,
but he warned that there would have to be lump sum guar-
antees from the home clubs. The New Zealanders turned the
offer down.

Among the first players to be offered a place on the tour
was Shrewsbury himself, but he wrote to Shaw (in residence
at Sheffield Park) in the spring of 1891: 'Dear Alfred, Please
excuse me not replying before to your letter; the reason is I
have been thinking the matter over very carefully, and the
more I go thoroughly into it, the greater the difficulties that
present themselves. Had you been staying at home (Shaw
was to travel as manager of the team) to look after the business, I might then have had a fair chance of considering what
recompense would have recouped me for being away from
here for about eight months. As you are well aware, our
business is now on the turning point and I am pleased to say
in the right direction, and through no other cause than that
of always being on the spot to direct and attend to all correspondence and to see that nothing is left unattended to. During
this winter and more especially the last few weeks (Shrewsbury had spent the previous month as coach at Edgbaston)
different things have occurred which clearly showed me, if
that was necessary, that one of us, as far as possible, should
keep an eye on the business ... Our experience of leaving
managers in possession is a very painful and expensive one,
and clearly shows our interests can only be looked after by
ourselves. At the same time I am not ungrateful of the high
honour Lord Sheffield has conferred upon me by inviting me
to become one of his team ... We had nine of the men off
work last week with influenza and I have had a bad cold now
for several weeks and am anxiously waiting for plenty of
warm weather.'

During his coaching engagement at Edgbaston, Shrewsbury watched over the development of Dick Lilley, who was
later to become a distinguished wicketkeeper-batsman for
both Warwickshire and England. In 1912 Lilley wrote his

autobiography and was full of praise for the skill Shrewsbury used when coaching the young Warwickshire players. In fact Shrewsbury's coaching apparently transformed the county side and to an extent must have been responsible for Warwickshire's promotion to first-class status three years later.

Lilley tells how Shrewsbury insisted on travelling home from Birmingham to Nottingham each night, rather than staying the week in Birmingham and Lilley says that the reason for this was that Shrewsbury was unable to sleep away from his own bed. This indeed was probably the reason Shrewsbury gave to Lilley, but one suspects that Shrewsbury returned every day to Nottingham to keep a strict eye on the business transactions of his firm – for a man who was not keen on sleeping away from the Queen's Hotel, he spent a terrible lot of time in Australia!

Notts opened their 1891 programme at the beginning of May with a match against second-class Derbyshire and a ten-wicket victory was obtained with Shrewsbury making 77 and 16 not out. The first serious encounter came at Whitsuntide. Notts failed on their first innings and the follow-on was enforced. Gunn and Dixon fought back, but Surrey still won by five wickets – Shrewsbury was out twice without achieving double figures. He failed again at Lord's in the second county match – Notts lost by 49 runs. The county's depressing form was reversed in the home game with Yorkshire; Billy Barnes recovered his all-round skill, hit a century and took 4 for 16 in the first innings. Shrewsbury on the other hand was caught behind the wicket before he had scored. His sequence of single figures continued against Lancashire, but another all-round display by Barnes produced victory by seven wickets. Yet another single figure innings for poor Arthur at Hove – his tally of first-class innings for Notts in 1891 now read: 2 and 8; 2 and 6; 0; 9 and 7; 6.

On 10 July his luck changed at last, and in the second innings against Sussex he hit 165, adding with William Gunn 312 for the second wicket. His terrible struggle through the first half of 1891 was banished and his scores for the rest of the summer for Notts were: 165; 59; 75 and 2; 82 and 5; 67; 178; 94; 21 and 6.

The last four games of the season were ruined by rain, so Notts had little opportunity to profit from Shrewsbury's success. Notts suffered two defeats by an innings, one of which was at the hands of the old rivals Surrey, but owing to an injured hand Shrewsbury could not bat in either match.

Notts ended the season fourth in the Championship, but they never challenged for first place, which went again to Surrey by a large margin. In the absence of a touring team from Australia, Gentlemen v Players at Lord's was the principal fixture of the summer. Staged as usual at the beginning of July, it came during Shrewsbury's black period and the press criticised his selection. Shrewsbury opened the innings and carried his bat right through for 81 out of 167 all out. Wisden's report noted: 'His play was far better than any other living batsman could have shown against the same bowling on the same wicket.' The weather was wet throughout the game and Shrewsbury's innings was interrupted several times by rain. The Gentlemen had the assistance of the Australian bowler Ferris, who had emigrated to England, as well as Sammy Woods, the Cambridge blue, then at the height of his bowling power.

Lord Sheffield's team, captained by W. G. Grace and managed by Alf Shaw, left England at the end of September. Apart from Shrewsbury, the only major cricketer to decline an invitation was William Gunn, and for similar reasons. Illingworth, Shrewsbury's suggestion as agent, proved a poor choice, though Shrewsbury, on hearing the news from Shaw, quickly put his finger on the trouble: 'I am not at all surprised re Illingworth. The mistake Lord Sheffield made was paying him in advance, as when he had nothing to receive, he bolted.'

Reading the reports of Lord Sheffield's first few matches, Shrewsbury learnt that the Australians seemed to have recovered their enthusiasm for the game and he began to think seriously about prompting another tour. This was quite natural as Shaw and Shrewsbury had a good number of business contacts in Australia and these needed to be maintained, but Shrewsbury made the quite extraordinary suggestion to Shaw that the latter ought to sound out the Melbourne Club with regard to a joint-promotion. Only three years before, the Melbourne Club had been the arch-enemy. Searching for an English sponsor, Shrewsbury met with Nottingham businessman, John Robinson, who was also the father of a young amateur Notts player, Sandford Robinson.

Shrewsbury mentioned Robinson to Shaw, but had considerable doubts: 'By what I can make out he (John Robinson) appears rather mean considering his great wealth, as he stopped over 5 per cent on that bill of ours, which comprised charges for Sandford's luggage. Turner (Notts CCC secretary) tells me he has never given a penny to the Castle Club since he has been a member. I only mention this to show what kind of a man he is, so that you might, if necessary, know how to deal with him.' In the same letter Shaw was told to try and sort out McShane, 'who is no doubt a rogue at heart'. It is not recorded whether Shaw had any better luck than Illingworth the previous year.

The English side did well enough until the first Test, which Australia won by 54 runs. It was about this time that Shaw told Shrewsbury that the costs of the tour were much in excess of Shrewsbury's estimate. Shrewsbury replied: 'I didn't know that Lord Sheffield had to pay for Grace's wife and family expenses in Australia. I thought he had repudiated that before leaving England. If he hadn't taken Grace out, Lord Sheffield would have been £3,000 better off at the end of the tour, and also had a better team. I told you what wine would be drunk by the Amateurs. Grace himself would drink enough to swim a ship.'

Jim Lillywhite, the partner of Shaw and Shrewsbury in their four tours, had fallen on hard times. It says much for Shrewsbury's compassion that he overlooked the large debt which Jim had left Shrewsbury to clear up, when he wrote to Shaw: 'I have been thinking that a fund could be raised in Australia on behalf of Jim. Lots of his friends that knew him when he was better off would be glad to subscribe a £5 or

£10. You could suggest it privately to Tommy Horan, Harry
Headley and Jack Conway, whom I am sure would do their
utmost on his behalf. Your name need not be mentioned, as
the players know he was indebted to us for a lot of money
and would guess the reason you had taken it up ... Jim was
well known in Sydney and Melbourne and if it is known that
he has scarcely the bare necessities of life in his old age a fair
sum should be obtained for him.' (Author's note: Lillywhite
was only 50 and was destined to outlive both Shaw and
Shrewsbury by more than 20 years.)

Lord Sheffield's Team returned home at the beginning of
May and Shrewsbury wrote to Bob Lewis, the manager of an
Adelaide sports outfitters: 'Was not at all surprised at the
result of the first two Test Matches (you would have won the
third as easily as you lost it, had you won the toss) as I never
considered Lord Sheffield's team a good one, being very far
from it. Am not saying this after the result, as I wrote to A.
Bannerman (the old Test cricketer) before a match was played
giving my opinion that a Combined Australian Team should
win. Should you see Alick (Bannerman), he will confirm this.
Of course I should like you to keep this private. In today's
paper a cable is sent from Adelaide saying that Lord Sheffield
is taking another team out to Australia – a stronger one –
next year and including myself. I don't think however Australia will ever see me again unless the inducement is much
greater than the previous offer.' The report of a possible
1892/3 tour by Lord Sheffield appeared in *The Times* from
their special correspondent in Melbourne, Gunn as well as
Shrewsbury being named as players. Nothing came of the
rumour, possibly because Lord Sheffield lost over £2,000
financing the 1891/2 visit. Shrewsbury's idea on expenditure was about half what the real figure came to – no doubt
due, at least in Shrewsbury's opinion, to the presence of five
amateurs in the side.

Looking at the few figures available for Shaw and Shrewsbury's business, it would appear that the firm was very
healthy. In 1890 turnover had increased by 14 per cent and
by a further 10 per cent in 1891, the slowing down being

due to the wet summer and the fact that a lot of cheap lines had been sold off at cost – presumably as a result of the move from Carrington Street. Shrewsbury mentioned to Shaw the possibility of obtaining a private loan of £1,000 from either Lord Sheffield or John Robinson, in order to expand the business, and this loan, Shrewsbury suggested, could raise the annual profit to about £1,000. Whether anything came of this plan is not known.

In April 1892, Shrewsbury undertook another four-week coaching engagement with Warwickshire at Edgbaston. He was paid £50 for this, with the proviso that he had Saturdays off. J. H. Edmiston of the West of Scotland CC asked Shrewsbury to take a team up to Glasgow for a three-day game. Shrewsbury quoted £120 for a first-class eleven, or £100 for an eleven composed of players such as Oliver Redgate, Walter Marshall, C. W. Wright etc., on the fringe of first-class cricket. The Scottish secretary declined the offer.

The opening first-class match of the 1892 Trent Bridge season was Alfred Shaw's benefit game, Lord Sheffield's tralian Team *versus* the Rest of England. Six seasons had gone by since Shaw was sacked from the Notts side and the general press comment was that the Notts Committee had been very dilatory regarding his benefit. As it was, rain put off the spectators and Shaw made little or nothing from the occasion. It served only to reinforce Shrewsbury's view of the weakness of Lord Sheffield's combination – they were dismissed for 89, whilst the Rest declared at 214 for 8.

Notts made a splendid start to the summer with five successive wins – against Sussex, Surrey, Lancashire, Middlesex and Somerset. This placed the county at the head of the Championship, though Surrey and Yorkshire, with four wins each out of five matches, were close on their heels. Shrewsbury made useful contributions in what were fairly low scoring matches, until the meeting with Middlesex at Lord's. In this match he was at the crease eight and a half hours and the report notes: 'His play was thoroughly characteristic, his unwearying defence continuing to the last. As an exhibition of watchful and scientific cricket his 212 was of course thoroughly worthy of the reputation of such a master of the art of batting.' It was in this match that Middlesex, having followed on 271 behind, made a spirited attempt to save the game, and with 30 minutes remaining still had five wickets to fall with Stoddart and Webbe batting well. Sandford Robinson, deputising as captain in place of J. A. Dixon, then called upon the veteran Notts wicketkeeper to bowl. Sherwin immediately dismissed Webbe and then Thesiger and with the other three wickets falling at the opposing end, Notts won by an innings with four minutes to spare. Richards comments: 'The Notts captain then decided, as a last resource, to put Sherwin on to bowl, himself taking the gloves. The spectators took this as a joke, and laughed to see the burly wicket-keeper prepare to deliver the ball.'

At the beginning of July came the two Gentlemen v Players fixtures. The match at Lord's came first and was a triumph for the Notts professionals, who comprised five of the Players' eleven. Shrewsbury scored 98 without a single chance, Gunn made 103 and Barnes 84. Barnes then took 6 wickets to force a follow-on by the amateurs and with more steady bowling from Dick Attewell, the side led by Sherwin won by an innings. At the Oval a ten-wicket victory was achieved, though this time most of the credit went to Arthur – he carried his bat through the completed innings, making 151 not out of the 325 total – the next best score was 36 by the Surrey batsman, Henderson. As at Lord's he did not give a chance in a stay lasting over five hours, the only faults being a 'few dangerous strokes in the slips'. His score was the highest made for the Players in this series to date.

In between the two Gentlemen v Players matches, a little family history was made at Hove, when Notts included Arthur Shrewsbury junior in their team to play Sussex. Arthur junior was the nephew of the great batsman, being the son of his brother William. The young colt made his debut three days after his eighteenth birthday and was a semi-professional with Notts Castle CC – alarmed by the loss of young talent, the Notts County Club had decided to allocate a sum of money to pay several young players, and these youngsters were signed to play with local Notts clubs. Arthur junior made a good impression, scoring 13 not out and 31 not out, but he was not to make his mark in County cricket.

The battle for the Championship was intense as July turned to August. Notts and Surrey were level – Notts had won seven and lost none, Surrey won eight and lost one, so each had seven points. When Notts travelled to London to play the August Holiday game at the Oval, the newspapers were full of the merits of the two counties; so much so that public opinion actually forced the Notts Committee to change their selected team, the amateur Charles Wright standing down in favour of Harry Daft.

No fewer than 34,010 spectators – the highest ever recorded – crammed into the Oval for the opening day and saw some thrilling cricket. Surrey were dismissed for 129 and at stumps Notts were 123 for 8. The erratic Shacklock took 8 Surrey wickets for 59, but the rejected Lockwood then took 8 for 67 for his adopted county – Shrewsbury was dismissed by a ball which broke in so unexpectedly that the batsman had ignored it. With the match so finely balanced over 32,000 came to watch the second day. Surrey scored 159 in their second innings, the main batting coming from Bobby Abel, who was brilliantly run out by Daft's throw from third man, and the captain John Shuter, who made 43 – he was well caught and bowled by Attewell running away to mid-off. Notts required 165. The crowd roared when Dixon was bowled by Lockwood without scoring and the noise increased as Shrewsbury was caught at slip for 10 – 12 for 2. Billy Barnes then joined Gunn and the pair steadily took the total to 106. At this point Barnes was bowled by Lockwood and four runs later Gunn went caught at the wicket. Wilfred Flowers was bowled with the total at 120, which meant 45 needed and five not very productive wickets left. Steady batting by Harry Daft however slowly took Notts to victory. The total attendance of 72,565 was a record for a three-day match.

On the crest of a wave, Notts beat Kent and Middlesex in the two following matches and thus had ten wins and no losses, compared with Surrey's eight wins and two losses. The

A group of cricketers in Adelaide during England's 1886/7 tour. *From left to right* Standing: W. H. Scotton and A. Shrewsbury. Seated in centre: A. Shaw.

The rugby football team that toured Australia and New Zealand in 1888. Arthur Shrewsbury is standing in the back row, third from the left.

Shaw and Shrewsbury's team that toured Australia, 1886/7, with Arthur Shrewsbury as captain. *From left to right* Standing: W. Flowers, A. Shrewsbury, G. Lohmann, W. Gunn, W. Barnes, J. M. Read. Seated: W. Bates, A. Shaw, J. Lillywhite, M. Sherwin, W. Scotton, R. G. Barlow. On the ground: J. Briggs.

The Nottinghamshire team of 1892. *From left to right* Standing: Shrewsbury, Barnes, Coxon (scorer), Attewell, Mr J. S. Robinson, Gunn, Shacklock. Seated: Sherwin, Mr O. Redgate, Mr J. A. Dixon, Mr C. W. Wright, Flowers. On the ground: Shrewsbury, Junior.

The Nottinghamshire team, taken in the match against Australia at Trent Bridge (8, 9 and 10 May 1902). The last photograph of Arthur Shrewsbury. *From left to right* Standing: H. Coxon (scorer), T. Wass, W. Gunn, A. Shrewsbury, T. Oates. Seated: J. Iremonger, Mr W. B. Goodacre, Mr A. O. Jones, Mr J. A. Dixon. On the ground: G. Anthony, J. Gunn, A. W. Hallam.

Amelia Love (1848–1924) sister of Arthur Shrewsbury.

Josiah Love, brother-in-law of Arthur Shrewsbury.

'The Limes', Gedling, as it looks today after modernisation.

The Queen's Hotel, Arkwright Street, Nottingham, home of Arthur Shrewsbury from 1869 to 1901.

Arthur Shrewsbury's tombstone in Gedling churchyard. The inscription reads: 'To the memory of Arthur Shrewsbury, for 28 years a member of the Notts County Cricket XI and a renowned cricketer. This monument was erected to perpetuate the esteem and regard of his relatives and friends. Born April 11th 1856, died May 19th 1903. "Our days on the earth are as but a shadow, and there is none abiding." '

William Shrewsbury (1879–1927), nephew of Arthur Shrewsbury, at the Shaw & Shrewsbury factory in about 1925.

Joseph Shrewsbury (1891–1954), nephew of Arthur Shrewsbury, at the factory in about 1935.

press commented on 11 August: 'The position of Notts has been so fortified by recent successes that the first place is practically assured, still there will probably be a keen competition for some of the other positions.'

Although Shrewsbury had made little contribution to the win over Surrey, his batting won the matches with both Kent – he carried his bat through the completed first innings, 111 out of 226 – and Middlesex. There was rather a curious incident in the Kent match. With the last two Kent batsmen at the wicket, Kent still needed two to avoid the follow on. Patterson, the Kent captain, actually walked out and spoke to the batsmen instructing them to throw away the last wicket next ball. This was overheard by the bowler, Dick Attewell, who then delivered a ball so off course that it went for four wides and thwarted Patterson's plan.

Shrewsbury hit another hundred in the next match at Cheltenham, where a stubborn innings from W. G. Grace gave Gloucester a draw. It was the Notts batsman's fifth hundred of the season and with 1,226 runs to date he had not only the best average, but also the highest aggregate.

Notts proceeded to Taunton, for their first ever match on that ground and totally against form were given an innings defeat by Somerset; from there they went to Old Trafford where a second innings defeat was suffered. Suddenly, from being certain champions, there had been a dramatic turn of events, for rivals Surrey won two matches and thus went two points ahead in the table. Since Notts could only draw their final match, due to rain, and Surrey completed their programme with another win, the final championship table does not reveal the exciting final fortnight of the summer, for Notts finished three points below Surrey:

	P	W	L	D	Pts
1. Surrey	16	13	2	1	11
2. Notts	16	10	2	4	8
3. Somerset	16	8	5	3	3

For the third successive season Shrewsbury headed the first-class batting table and by some odd quirk was the only professional in the top seven, Gunn coming eighth with an average 12 runs below Shrewsbury.

The year 1892 was a good year for the firm of Shaw and Shrewsbury. The factory was enlarged and more staff recruited. The manufacture of cricket balls was increased – some idea of the quantity sold can be gauged by the fact that in South Australia alone the firm reckoned on selling 100 dozen. Shrewsbury was a careful manager; when Mordecai Sherwin suggested that his son, having served a three-year apprenticeship in bat manufacture, deserved a rise from 22/6 per week to 30/-, Shrewsbury stated that he was unable to oblige 'without sustaining a great loss'.

There was obviously some concern at the firm over the growing rival company of Gunn and Moore. Shrewsbury wrote to Shaw telling him that on no account should Dick Attewell be allowed to see details of the firms Shaw and Shrewsbury dealt with overseas, because Attewell would only go straight to Gunn and Moore and give them the information.

The winter of 1892/3 was a quiet one for cricket followers. The main interest, since Lord Sheffield's proposed second Australian tour came to nothing, was the selection of the Australian side to visit England in 1893. Notts had granted Shrewsbury the use of Trent Bridge for a benefit match and he arranged for the Australian team to play against a side he selected. The Notts Committee thus broke with tradition, since all previous benefits granted by the Committee had been for players who had retired from first-class cricket.

As in the previous two summers, Shrewsbury began 1893 with a run of small scores. Notts experimented with Gunn opening the innings with Shrewsbury in the Easter Colts Match and the pair had a successful partnership of 116. They were tried again in the non-first-class match with Warwickshire and had opening stands of 145 and 85, but in Championship games the innovation was not very successful and after a few trials Dixon returned to partner Shrewsbury.

Large crowds came to Trent Bridge for the Surrey Whitsun game; Surrey's new discovery, the fast bowler Tom Richard-

son, not only dismissed Shrewsbury twice, but nearly everyone else – 14 for 145 were his match figures and Notts lost
by three wickets. Shrewsbury's first big innings for Notts
came at Hove in early June. With Gunn he had yet another
massive partnership at the expense of the Sussex attack, the
pair adding 274 for the second wicket. Shrewsbury made 164
and Gunn 156. The later batsmen continued the run spree,
which ended with a total of 674, the second highest ever
made in a Championship match, and the highest ever by
Notts. Unfortunately the Notts bowling was unable to remove
Sussex twice and the game was drawn. After Shrewsbury's
failure against Richardson, the press immediately jumped to
the conclusion that he was getting too old to cope with fast
bowling. Shrewsbury's reply was a splendid 148 against Lancashire, who possessed, in Arthur Mold, a very dangerous
fast bowler.

His benefit came round at the end of June and he gathered
a most representative England side, which beat the Australians by an innings. Virtually everyone on the winning team
made a decent contribution. The captain, W. G. himself, hit
49, Stoddart 94, Gunn 64, Palairet, the young Somerset batsman, 71, and Shrewsbury, coming in at number five, carried
out his bat for 52. The Australians were bowled out by Bobby
Peel, the Yorkshire left-arm spinner. About 6,000 attended
on each of the first two days. Shrewsbury received about
£200 from the match itself and a further £300 from subscription lists.

Chosen for both the Gentlemen v Players fixtures, he was
badly injured when batting at the Oval, being hit on the head
by a ball from Ernest Smith, the Yorkshire fast bowler. He
continued his innings, but, having scored 25 more runs, was
bowled, and as the pain grew worse he left the match at the
end of the first day and returned home to Nottingham. Considering this injury it was surprising that he returned to London three days later for the return match at Lord's to face the
Essex cricketer, Charles Kortright, regarded by many as the
fastest bowler ever to play in county cricket. The Wisden
report comments: 'The feature of the innings was the superb

batting of Shrewsbury, who went in first and stayed till the
total reached 165. Out of this number he made no fewer than
88 ... He played Kortright with perfect skill, scoring with the
utmost certainty whenever the fast bowler pitched at all
short.'

The following week came the first of three Test Matches
against the Australians. W. G. Grace could not play owing to
injury and Stoddart led England. He won the toss, but with
a soft pitch and hot sun took a gamble in deciding to bat. He
opened with Shrewsbury, with the critics thinking England
would do well to reach 150. The great Notts batsman however was equal to the demands placed upon him. He remained
at the wicket for four hours and ten minutes, scoring 106,
an innings 'marked by extreme patience, unfailing judgment,
and a mastery over the difficulties of the ground, of which
probably no other batsman would have been capable.'
Shrewsbury's partner for a large part of his innings was the
young amateur and Cambridge captain, F. S. Jackson, who
hit out, was dropped three times, but made 91. England hit
334 instead of the predicted 150. Australia were all out for
269. In the second innings Shrewsbury again hit the highest
score for his side, 81, and partnered by Gunn added 152 for
the second wicket. Stoddart declared to set Australia 300 in
225 minutes, but the rain arrived and prevented the final
innings taking place.

Between these successes, Notts played two matches against
Yorkshire, drawing one and losing the second. Shrewsbury
did little in either, in fact in one innings he had the miserable
experience of being run out off the first ball of the innings. It
was not until the eve of the second Test that Shrewsbury
managed another major score for his county. His 124 at
Canterbury enabled Notts to reach 336 against Kent, but the
Notts bowlers were unable to take full advantage of a first
innings lead of 134 and the game was drawn – a pattern
that was becoming all too familiar to Notts supporters.

W. G. Grace was fit for the second Test, played at the Oval.
England batted first on a perfect wicket and every one of the
batsmen, except for Gunn, hit individual fifties. Shrewsbury

made 66 and the total reached 483. Lockwood and Briggs, the two Notts-born bowlers, skittled Australia out for 91, 'a wretchedly poor score, considering the wicket was fast and true', and though the tourists fought back when following on, England achieved an innings victory. The third and last Test, at Old Trafford, like the first, was drawn. Gunn was England's star with the only hundred of the game. Shrewsbury made 12 and 19 not out. He ended the series at the top of the England batting averages with 284 runs, average 71·00.

Shrewsbury and Notts ended their Championship season, also at Old Trafford, with a considerable flourish. Victory over Lancashire by nine wickets included Shrewsbury's innings of 101 and 23 not out. The county however had had a very modest summer. With just five wins, against seven losses, they were sixth of the nine counties.

William Gunn headed the general first-class averages and Shrewsbury had to be content with fourth place behind the amateurs Stoddart and Jackson, though only two runs separated the first four.

Whilst Shrewsbury still demonstrated his ability to be the equal of any batsman in England, his erstwhile friend, Will Scotton, had gradually lost his form and faded from the county scene. He played his last match for Notts in 1890 and his final first-class match for MCC the following summer, though he continued on the ground staff at Lord's in 1892 and 1893. He became increasingly depressed, his marriage broke up and the happy days of cricket in Beeston with Arthur Shrewsbury and his other young contemporaries were long gone. He had fallen out with most of his old friends, George Hearne being one of the few to stick by him. On 9 July 1893 he committed suicide by cutting his own throat in the bedroom of his lodgings near Lord's. It would appear that Shrewsbury was unaffected by his death, since his great hundred at Lord's in the Gentlemen v Players match was compiled on the Monday, Scotton having died on the previous Saturday.

In the autumn of 1893 the problems with Trimmings,

which Shrewsbury had forecast six years before, finally came
to a head. Trimmings had corrupted Bates, the man Shaw
had engaged whilst Shrewsbury was in Australia. Bates had
resigned from the firm early in 1893 and returned to work
for Daft's emporium, taking with him a full list of all Shaw
and Shrewsbury's overseas contacts. Due to Bates' management, or as Shrewsbury described it, mis-management, Daft's
firm went bankrupt in the summer of 1893 and was bought
up by the London sports outfitters, F. H. Ayres, who retained
Bates as manager. To impress his new masters Bates began
writing to all Shaw and Shrewsbury's customers enclosing
lists of sports goods for sale at prices he knew to be below
Shaw and Shrewsbury's.

It was not long before Shrewsbury became aware of this
and began to wonder how Bates could undercut Shaw and
Shrewsbury and still make a fair profit. A careful check by
Shrewsbury quickly uncovered the swindle. Trimmings, in
league with Bates, was not only stealing materials from Shaw
and Shrewsbury and passing them on to Bates, but was also
getting some of the employees of Shaw and Shrewsbury to
stay after hours and manufacture extra goods which were
also to be passed on to Bates, though Shrewsbury exposed
this before any finished products could be removed from the
factory. Trimmings was charged with theft and sentenced to
one month's hard labour – he also returned £30 worth of
cricket willow which he had stolen.

Shrewsbury in a long letter to his South Australian business friend, Bob Lewis, wrote: 'We have been very unfortunate in our managers, both in the factory and the shop. You
will naturally say, well why don't you look after your own
business. The fact is, we have been away cricketing a great
deal during the summer, which unfortunately for us has been
taken advantage of. This won't occur in future, as I don't
contemplate playing much cricket during the coming summer.'

The final sentence is interesting. The letter was written in
February 1894 and, as it happened, Shrewsbury did not play
in a single first-class match in 1894, though the reason given

in the cricket press for his continued absence was asthma and bronchitis. Perhaps illness was a diplomatic excuse for the general public, but it can hardly have convinced the people of Nottingham, as Shrewsbury was seen quite often in the Saturday matches of Notts Castle CC and indeed scored several hundreds for that club.

No sooner had Trimmings been released from prison than he went into partnership with R. M. Pett of Nottingham and the firm began to manufacture cricket bats under the style 'The National Bat Co.' Shrewsbury was very anxious that this new firm would not take business from him and no doubt he was looking over his shoulder at the continued expansion of Gunn and Moore. The correspondence to the various overseas markets he had developed increased rapidly in 1894. Among the better known names with whom he was in correspondence are Sid Gregory, who was thinking of opening a sports outfitters in Sydney, and Charley Turner, the great bowler, who ran another sports business. Writing to the latter, Shrewsbury begins a letter: 'We have sent you 2 dozen very fine bats indeed, which should only be used by experienced players.'

Anxious to keep the overseas shop managers sweet, Shrewsbury, in a typical letter, this one addressed to James Witt of Dunedin, wrote: 'Any little thing you would like us to send out for your personal use – which we would ask your acceptance of with our compliments – i.e. a pair of hand-sewn boots, which are manufactured here, home-cured ham, which is a luxury I never had the privilege of tasting when in Australia or NZ, or any other thing you would prefer, would be of very little trouble to us, and could be forwarded with other goods.'

In August Shrewsbury received a letter from South Africa, the writer being George Lohmann, the Surrey and England cricketer. Shrewsbury replied: 'Dear George, Yours of July 23rd recd allright and I can assure you I was pleased to have a line, and to hear your health has so greatly improved. (Due to illness, Lohmann had been forced to retire from county cricket and was living with the South African cricket patron,

John Logan.) Trust it may continue to do so, and that before long we may see you in your old form taking part in matches over here ... Stoddart is taking a trip to the Colonies, *as an Amateur of course* with an English team and by so doing has robbed Gunn and myself from taking a trip there with Lord Sheffield's Team, who intended going out this fall – he only intended playing 3 international matches and then coming home, but this of course wouldn't suit the Melbourne and Sydney authorities and enough new members could not be enrolled to see one match at each place – so they boycotted Lord Sheffield's trip and for the good of cricket and their own pockets invited Stoddart to take a team out on similar lines, with many amateurs who are hard up, and yet who continue to get a nice round cheque each season out of cricket. Hear Mr Read (the Surrey amateur batsman) is going to have a benefit and I should not be surprised if he got £1,000. (Barnes will, if he is lucky, get between £300 and £400.) The sooner you arrange about yours the better for you and the longer you delay the worse for you.'

On the benefits which Shrewsbury mentions, Barnes actually received £350 and the so-called amateur, Read, £720. With regard to the proposed tour by Lord Sheffield, presumably Shrewsbury had been made an offer by his lordship which he could not refuse and was therefore a trifle upset when Lord Sheffield's ideas were cancelled in favour of Stoddart's enlarged tour proposals.

An interesting note in one 1894 letter throws light on the keenness of collectors of cricketana, even at this early date. Pratt Green of Malvern writes to Shrewsbury requesting a bat and the cricketer replies, 'Re bat of mine. I will send you one I had put upon one side for the coming summer. I have not an old one left, and when they are completely done up, and not worth a penny, as regards their practical value, I dispose of them to a gentleman at a very good figure, who has already a number of them, with all the scores I have obtained, with match and date, inscribed upon them.'

A begging letter arrived in September 1894 from Mrs Lillywhite in Chichester. Shrewsbury replied:

Yours to hand. In reply I should like to give you a few particulars as briefly as possible, how matters stand and how the present position of affairs has been brought about, and who is responsible for them. The last cricket tour we lost, the three of us, about £800 each, the football tour about £100 each. In addition to this I had a letter of credit for £200, most of which was *lent* to your husband in addition to about £60 or more for cricketing gear, which I disposed of. This amount should be repaid to us, in addition to the other liabilities incurred. Had Mr Lillywhite mentioned to us, which he certainly ought to have done before taking the last trip, that he was not in a position to incur any losses, then the tour would not have taken place. Personally it has made a difference to me of about £1,800 as I could have gone out with the team which the Melbourne Club took out. You can't imagine the serious loss we have sustained in our business, through not being able at the time to meet the just demands of the players that went out with us, and also in many other ways.

Suppose we had acted in a similar manner to Mr L., the players, who had done their best for our interest, would absolutely have received not one penny of the money they were entitled to. He allowed one of the footballers to overdraw to the extent of £60 or £70, knowing, as in the case of the money I lent him, that he was not in a position to pay one penny of it back ... Where has all the money gone to from the various trips Mr L. has taken to the Colonies. Not taking into account the one with Dr Grace (in 1873/4), he has been out five times besides. He made a lot of money the second time, the third £1,300 or £1,400, the fourth about £700 or £800.

The demands we have had to meet have crippled us a great deal in our business and we have only one man to thank for it. He went out fully prepared to drag us down, if the trip was not successful, having in the meantime made arrangements to secure himself against harm. I have thought it my duty to reply to your letter, and although the figures quoted may not be entirely accurate, they are not far off the mark.

I beg to remain, Yours Truly,
Arthur Shrewsbury.

There is no further reference to Lillywhite in Shrewsbury's correspondence, but in view of the letter above, some remarks made by J.C. Bristow-Noble, who interviewed Lillywhite

shortly before the latter died, are worthy of repetition:
'Though in receipt of a comfortable income derived from in-
vestments, Lillywhite chose to work up to within a few weeks
of his death. This old man ... actually passed the last
twenty-eight years of his life (i.e. 1902–29) working chiefly
in a stone quarry, quarrying stone.'

Stoddart's Team duly went to Australia in the autumn of
1894 and having won the first Test were again successful in
the second, about which Shrewsbury commented: 'The Australians ought to have won, if the gale and money had not
stood in the way, as they threw a strong point away in
allowing the wicket to be rolled on the Saturday night, after
the finish of play and no doubt all day Sunday. Had it been
Lord Sheffield's Team or Lord Hawke's, such a proceeding
would not have been tolerated. It would have been impossible
to have rolled the bad places down on the Monday morning
ten minutes before the match and in all probability the match
would have been all over on that day ... Such a proceeding
would never for one moment have been allowed in England
in so important a match, no matter what difference it would
have made to the gate.' In the match England were dismissed
for 75, then Australia for 123. At this point the weekend
rolling to which Shrewsbury strongly objected took place.
England went in to bat a second time, reaching a total of
475, Stoddart making 173. Australia made 333 in the fourth
innings. The second and third days of the match were the
New Year Holiday and the profit or loss on the tour almost
hinged on the public attendance on these days. In the event
36,000 people came over the two days and about £1,400
was taken at the gate. The series ended with England winning
three Tests to two.

9 County Cricket and a Business Quarrel

Nottinghamshire's 1894 season was less successful than its predecessor. With four wins against eight losses, the county fell to seventh place. Apart from Gunn, the batting was desperately weak. Barnes and Dixon did virtually nothing in Championship games. A lot of new faces were brought in, but none achieved much – even Jack Sharpe, the Notts-born Surrey player, now rejected by his adopted county, was recruited, but failed. It was therefore with some urgency that G. M. Royle, on the Notts Committee, wrote to Shrewsbury in February 1895, asking about the batsman's intentions for the coming summer. Shrewsbury replied, 'I shall no doubt play cricket next summer if my health and business permit, but as to the time I am likely to begin, it depends very much on the spring. You see I am handicapped to a certain extent, as I am not allowed to go in for practice early, and by the time warm weather sets in, the season is well advanced, and then it is necessary to have at least six weeks practice after that to get thoroughly into anything like form and condition – the older one gets, the more practice is required to loosen the muscles etc.'

It is difficult to know what interpretation to put on this letter. Who would not allow Shrewsbury to practise early? Presumably his doctors, but it is known from his later diary that he went to the indoor nets almost throughout the winter. A note in *Cricket* for 18 April states: 'Arthur Shrewsbury, who it was hoped would be able to play regularly once more, has been ill again recently, and it is doubtful whether he can be reckoned upon.' The hypochondria which was to take an increasing hold upon him must have played its part at this

time. His office letter files show that he attended regularly to
the business in the early months of 1895, so whatever the
ailment it did not confine him to bed.

The illness may well have been further 'shop problems'.
Yet another of Shaw and Shrewsbury's managers left under
a cloud in April, 1895 and Shrewsbury once more circular-
ised his customers, warning them that they might receive
literature from Clarke, trying to undercut Shaw and Shrewsbury. The ill-fated Bates had been dismissed from the manager-
ship of the Daft-Ayres cricket outfitters and gone into a
'small cheap jack place of business combining shaving and
haircutting with his sports business.'

Saturday 8 June was Shrewsbury's first match day of 1895.
He hit an unbeaten hundred for Notts Castle against Pilsley.
He had more or less promised Wilfred Flowers to play for
Flowers' benefit, Notts v Lancashire on June 17, 18 and 19,
and this was indeed the scene of his reappearance in county
cricket. The match turned out to be a disaster for Notts.
Arthur Mold bowled the home county out twice on the
second day for 35 and 122. Both times Shrewsbury was
dismissed by Mold very cheaply. There was some newspaper
talk about Shrewsbury leaving Nottingham and qualifying for
Sussex. The appearance in the 1894 Sussex ranks of Alfred
Shaw and his achievements after being absent from county
cricket for so many years, allied with some wishful thinking,
seem to have produced Shrewsbury's rumoured departure for
Sussex, but there seems nothing concrete to it.

It was four weeks before Shrewsbury re-joined the county
eleven. This time he hit 143, without offering a chance. In
the following game he reached another hundred and
although Notts were easily beaten, Shrewsbury with 29 and
111 had the highest score in both innings. Notts were suffering their worst ever season. In 1895 the Championship was
expanded from nine counties to fourteen; in mid-July, with
ten of their eighteen fixtures played, the county stood twelfth,
having won just two games.

The next game was at Lord's against Middlesex. Shrewsbury made 29 out of the all out Notts total of 109, then hurt

his hand fielding and missed the two following fixtures, which brought the calendar round to the August Bank Holiday. The wretched performances of Notts continued and, of the batting against Surrey, it need only be said that Shrewsbury made the highest individual score in each innings – 23 and 13. It is too depressing to catalogue the remaining matches of the season, all lost, bar one draw. About the only bright spot was the batting of Shrewsbury, who ended the summer with a Championship average of 48 – Gunn was on 33 and Flowers next on 23. The bowling was almost entirely in the hands of Dick Attewell.

A series of letters in the winter of 1895/6 reveals one of Arthur's great weaknesses – a passion for Turkish Delight. Alfred Shaw had been on a cruise with Lord Sheffield and among the ports of call was Constantinople. Here Alfred purchased some Turkish Delight with almonds and brought the present back to Nottingham for Arthur. Shrewsbury located a London firm which specialised in the importation of Turkish Delight and wrote asking to purchase some. A definite order was made. Six weeks passed and Shrewsbury wrote again to the firm: 'When O when will it be? Had no idea when order was placed for Delight, I should have to wait until now. Can you inform me to three or four months when it is likely to be sent?' The Delight finally arrived in April, but the invoice confused Arthur: 'We can scarcely understand the enclosed invoice. In the prices you gave us at Nottingham for Turkish Delight, this was quoted in 2 lb drums at 36/- per cwt, with an addition of 2/9d per cwt for 20 per cent nut with it. The enclosed is quoted at 42/3d per cwt. This must be a mistake. We notice you have sent more than one cwt, but this won't matter.' The firm then explained that the cost was 38/9d per cwt with nuts, but the freight charge from Constantinople was 1/6d per cwt and the dock charges an additional 2/- per cwt. Shrewsbury thought the dock charges rather heavy, but paid the account, thanking the firm for its courtesy.

The 1896 cricket season was approaching. Unlike the previous year, Shrewsbury was not banned from pre-season practice and went often to the indoor nets in Beeston. J. A.

Dixon, the Notts captain, wrote to Shrewsbury asking if he, Dixon, might join the indoor practice and Shrewsbury replied:

Dear Mr Dixon,

Yours of 5th to hand, for which I am much obliged. We should feel greatly honoured by your company upon any of the days we visit Beeston, and have no doubt you would learn more agst our Bowling, which as you know, has more variety in it, than the stereotype come-as-you-like-it, sort of Bowling of Attewell and Flowers. I want you to allow me to pay my proportionate share of the expense of the room, and feel that, without you do this, I am rather an intruder. Will you please mention this to Green, whom I wish to thank along with yourself for the privilege accorded, at the same time, I trust you will, without any hesitation, accede to what I ask.

Yours sincerely,
Arthur Shrewsbury

The letter so nicely illustrates the relationship between the senior Notts professional and the captain. Shrewsbury was starting his 22nd season with Notts and Dixon's county career, apart from a few scattered appearances, was some nine summers old. Dixon had offered to pay the full rental of the barn, which was used as the indoor net.

Just before the season got under way, Shrewsbury had more trouble from his most recently sacked manager, who was trying to persuade Shaw and Shrewsbury customers to leave the firm. Shrewsbury wrote a standard letter to all his major clients: 'W. Clarke, our former manager, is now at Birmingham in a retail shop. After leaving us he occupied his time in betting on horse racing, until he obtained employment.'

The Australians toured England in 1896. Shrewsbury played against them twice before the first Test and failed in both matches and as was now usual did not really run into form until the middle of the season. Several times he seemed well set only to lose his wicket unexpectedly – in the Notts

game against the Australians beginning June 25, he made
39 and 23, both innings being described as excellent. His first
major success came against Gloucestershire at Trent Bridge.
Opening with A. O. Jones, the young Cambridge blue, who
had displaced Dixon as Shrewsbury's partner, he held the side
together on the first afternoon, when by stumps Notts were
129 for 5 in reply to Gloucester's 168, Shrewsbury being 39
not out. On the second morning, Shrewsbury hit out to reach
an unbeaten 125, when Notts were dismissed for 277. His
only other hundred of 1896 came against Kent. After helping
Jones to put on 223 for the first wicket, Shrewsbury was 133
not out at the close of the first day, with Notts 326 for 5. In
the end he was dismissed for 172, having batted seven hours.
The bowling was not sharp enough to dismiss Kent twice and
the game, like several others during the summer, was drawn
because of this. Notts ended the season in the middle of the
table, which was certainly an improvement on the immediate
past, but they never remotely challenged the first four counties – Yorkshire, Lancashire, Middlesex and Surrey. Notts'
weakness was very simply illustrated in the Championship
bowling averages: Attewell 86 wickets, average 14·55 first;
Brown 43 wickets, average 21·13 second. The fact that Sam
Brown, in his 40th year, was the second best Notts bowler
was evidence enough of Notts' problems. Brown, born in Kimberley, Notts, had played for Cheshire from 1882 to 1895,
when the Cheshire County Cricket Club collapsed; Brown was
then invited by Notts to make his debut for his native county
– the unending supply of young talent which had kept Notts
and quite a number of other counties in bowlers for forty
years had dried up. After years of dithering the Notts Committee finally moved with the times and for the start of the
1897 season created a ground-staff of young cricketers for
Trent Bridge.

The Australians played three Tests against England in
1896, the home country winning the series two to one. No
doubt the absence of Charley Turner from the touring team
helped England – Turner owed money to Shaw and Shrewsbury for cricket goods supplied and Shrewsbury was certain

that Turner's non-appearance was due entirely to the number of debts he had acquired in England in 1893.

In the spring of 1897, Shrewsbury received a letter from an unexpected quarter and replied:

Dear Colonel

Yours of Feb 22 duly received and I was greatly surprised to have a line from you. Very pleased to hear you are getting on so well and that cricket has not altogether lost all its old charm for you. Am not surprised at you getting plenty of runs, neither am I surprised at you getting run out; that, I think, pretty frequently occurred when here ... Am sending you a bat through Dr Grace and hope you will get a lot of big scores with it. Don't blame the bat if you don't. Alfred is well and spends most of his time, when not with Lord Sheffield, at the factory here.

The letter was addressed to W. R. Gilbert, 7 Lincoln Avenue, Montreal, Canada. Gilbert, a cousin of W. G. Grace and a noted Gloucestershire county amateur cricketer, had been shipped off to Canada after being prosecuted for stealing from the clothes of fellow cricketers in the pavilion dressing room some ten years previously.

Business was again improving. The manufacture of cricket balls had been improved and Shaw and Shrewsbury balls were now being used in first-class county matches, indeed W. G. Grace (boasted Shrewsbury to a customer) insisted on them rather than cricket balls made in the traditional area in Kent. On the bat business, Shrewsbury noted: 'We have a magnificent stock of willow, more than double the quantity we have ever had before, and from what we can see are likely to require it.'

The 1897 season was one during which cricket interest rested entirely on the Championship – the tour by the Phila-delphians was not followed to any extent by the public. With the new ground-staff, Notts played quite a number of extra matches against non-first-class counties and although Shrewsbury did not play in many of these additional games, he appeared in all but one of the Championship contests and was reliability itself, averaging 38 in 21 completed innings, though his highest score was only 83. Wisden commented: 'Though it would of course be an exaggeration to say he was as fine a bat as in his greatest days, he was still quite good enough to play for England.'

Shrewsbury proved this correct when he made his only non-Notts first-class appearance of the summer in the major Gentlemen v Players match at Lord's. The report of the match in the magazine *Cricket* notes 'The feature of the first day's cricket was the batting of Shrewsbury, polished as ever; during his long innings he hardly ever made a mistake; his timing was wonderful to watch, and his strokes all round the wicket left nothing to be desired. No one – even a man who cannot understand what there can be to see in mere "style" – could have described his innings of 125 as slow.' He batted 220 minutes for his runs. The *Daily Telegraph* adds the following: 'Not the least remarkable of his qualities is his economy of force. Even when he does hit the ball to the ring he never seems to greatly exert himself. A flexible wrist and perfect timing do all that is necessary. No one accommodates himself more readily than Shrewsbury to varying conditions of ground. The wicket at Lord's yesterday was extremely fast, and one noticed that he played forward a great deal more than he does on slower grounds, such as Trent Bridge. The most remarkable feature of his innings was the extraordinary skill with which he scored on the on side. Whenever the ball was pitched at all short away it went. Sometimes the batsman scored four, more often only a single, but the certainty of execution was always the same. It is a great treat to all who can enjoy the niceties of scientific batting to see Shrewsbury at his best; and that the crowd appreciated his skill was made clear by the cheers that constantly rewarded him during his innings.'

Stoddart's second team to Australia sailed from Tilbury on 17 September. Shrewsbury wrote to his broker in Australia regarding his gold shares: 'We have every confidence in your sound judgment and ability, and are well content to leave matters entirely in your hands, knowing you will do the best for us. We don't belong to that fortunate class of individuals who whatever they touch or whatever speculation they may engage, turns out profitable. Perhaps however some time luck will change. Re: Cricket; no doubt the Indian Prince will be a great attraction in Stoddart's Team, although his cricket this year has been a long way inferior to last.' The Indian Prince was Ranjitsinhji, who had taken the cricket world by storm in 1896, easily topping the batting averages and being capped by England.

As Stoddart's Team was failing in Australia, Shaw and Shrewsbury were branching out into new lines. They took the sole agency in Australia for a Nottingham bicycle company and also wrote to Ceylon in the hope of dealing in tea on the wholesale market, though adding the postscript: 'Are there many firms who do cricket in Colombo, we do a little business there already?'

Contrary to his usual custom, Shrewsbury not only played in the Easter Colts trial at Trent Bridge, but immediately ran into form, hitting 71 against Derbyshire in the first county match and a week later 154 not out against Sussex at Hove – on the sea-side ground, he and Gunn had a partnership of 241, recalling memories of earlier triumphs. The pair, now approaching the veteran stage, had another three-figure stand in the return with Sussex, broken when Shrewsbury was run out at 126. Oddly he was run out twice in the following match against Yorkshire. Altogether Shrewsbury had an excellent summer – sixth in the batting averages with 45·14. On the Championship front, Notts in mid-season looked like winning the title, a situation which was causing the authorities much heart-burn. The system in vogue in 1898 was that positions in the table were decided by a percentage of wins to losses, with drawn matches ignored. Notts stood at the top, having won one match and drawn seven, thus having 100 per cent record. Happily for the administrators Notts went on to lose two matches and failed to obtain an additional win, so total embarrassment was saved – but that single success put Notts eighth of fourteen!

Shrewsbury went to Hastings for his summer holidays: 'I require 2 separate bedrooms and one private sitting room. Of course we should find ourselves in food, but cooking and washing would have to be included. I want a nice quiet place, where there are not a lot of people staying and where the apartments and cooking are good. The last place you obtained for us (in 1895) was fairly good, and what was rather important nice and quiet, the only objection being it was rather far from Hastings – though this did not matter very much – and they always turned the gas out at 11 o'clock each night, which was rather inconvenient after having been to a place of amusement for the evening. Of course candles could be used.'

One of the few adverse comments concerning Shrewsbury's batting was his use of pads as a second line of defence. Rait Kerr in his book 'The Laws of Cricket', stated: 'As we have seen the improvement in pitches enabled Arthur Shrewsbury to develop a new gospel of defensive batsmanship which soon made many converts. From about 1885 this technique involved an increasing use of the pads, which in a year or two was causing the deepest concern in the cricket world and as a result the reform of the lbw Law became the question of the hour.' In the 1880s the Law stated that, for the batsman to be given out, the ball had to pitch between wicket and wicket and in the opinion of the umpire would have hit the wicket. The MCC considered the position in 1888, but did not alter the Law, only issuing a statement saying that defending the wicket with the person rather than the bat was against the spirit of the game. This seemed to help for a few seasons, but by the turn of the century the problem had returned.

This is not the place for a detailed history of the lbw Law, but the fact that Rait Kerr singles out Shrewsbury as the innovator of a new batting style – apart from the 18th century players he is almost the only batsman named in the whole book – makes this remark worthy of explanation at least. Shrewsbury in fact earned himself a bad name, not on account of his own batting, but on account of his imitators, who while they employed his defensive methods were incapable of Shrewsbury's skill and judgment in attacking the loose ball and guiding it between the fieldsmen.

The Australians came on tour yet again in 1899. 'The

cricket season here is rapidly approaching,' Shrewsbury wrote to a friend in Australia, 'and great interest is being taken in the coming visit of the Australian Eleven. If they can hold their own in the Test Matches, the ground won't hold the people, and we have no doubt there is a lot of money in the venture. Here in Nottingham we are spending £4,000 on improvements on the ground, which will be equal to any in England.'

Trent Bridge was the venue of the first Test – the first such match ever played in Nottingham. William Gunn was the sole Notts representative in the drawn match, which was characterised by slow scoring. It is not known if Shrewsbury was invited to play, but later during the summer he wrote to his Australian friend: 'The Australian Team are doing remarkably well and should win or draw all the Test Matches with equal luck, as they appear to be a strong side, whilst ours was never weaker all round, more particularly in bowling. I was asked to play in the match commencing today (third Test at Headingley), but find continuous cricket much harder work than formerly and am only taking part in our County matches.' Rain ruined an interesting last day in the drawn third Test. Australia won the series with one win and four draws.

Shrewsbury had a quite excellent summer with Notts and closed the year fifth in the first-class averages, so at least on paper he deserved a place in the Test team; his highest score was 175 against Yorkshire at Bradford, but in the Bristol game against Gloucestershire he made 146 and with A. O. Jones created a new first wicket record partnership of 391 for Notts – in fact at that date there had been only one higher stand for the first wicket. In the period commencing 15 May, Shrewsbury had successive innings of 101 not out, 40, 146, 52, 114, 47, 69, 44, the best consecutive run of eight innings he had had through his long career. Notts still suffered from a surfeit of drawn games, and having only two wins, were tenth in the Championship.

During the winter of 1899/1900 he was in correspondence with W. A. J. West, the old county cricketer and umpire. 'My brother's name is off the list of umpires,' Shrewsbury wrote, 'but I notice all the old soldiers and strategists are left in a solid body. Some of these would be useful in South Africa (the Boer War was at its height). However I am pleased to see your name down, although I have been the chief victim of your over conscientiousness and I should think you have made a difference in my average of about 10 or 15 runs each year. I think I am selected by the umpires as a sample to experiment upon, as last year L. Hall (the ex-Yorkshire batsman) gave me out at the Oval – lbw – when I was well in and looked like getting 150 not out (he made 64). However he did the needful afterwards by apologizing very humbly for his mistake, which is more than some people I know do, who make as great blunders. Am pleased to say my health, as far as I know, is all right and I hope to have the pleasure of meeting you on the green sward again next summer. You will see I am having a Complimentary Benefit, don't you think I am fortunate?'

Arthur's brother, William, had joined the first-class umpires' list in 1896. In 1900, the MCC had a grand clear-out and struck no less than seventeen umpires off the list, including William Shrewsbury. Arthur presumably believed the wrong men had been retained, though L. Hall was also struck off.

The 1900 season soon arrived. Shrewsbury did not play in the Easter Colts game, held in mid-April, and at the beginning of May he wrote to the Notts Secretary:

Dear Mr Turner,

I thought it best to write to you in time so that you could obtain someone in my place for the MCC match next Wednesday; I am sorry to say I shall have to decline to play, the weather being too cold to turn out. I don't want to run any risks and have to stand down during the first half of the season, which would be a great disappointment to me, now that the warm weather is drawing so near. Shall be very pleased indeed when a change takes place.

Believe me to remain, faithfully yours,
Arthur Shrewsbury
P.S. Am taking it for granted I have been selected to play.

The postscript says almost as much as the letter itself.

A. O. Jones took over the captaincy of Notts in 1900. The most outstanding close fieldsman of his day, a fine opening batsman and a useful slow bowler, he was an inspiring leader and soon began putting Notts cricket back on its feet. Mainly due to his batting Notts won the first three of their county matches, which then brought them to the Whitsuntide game with Surrey – Shrewsbury had been granted half the net proceeds of the match as a testimonial. Unlike the last few meetings of the two counties, this game was closely fought, Surrey being set 261 to win in their last innings in about 230 minutes. Notts obtained early wickets, but their hopes were dashed by Lockwood who made 74 against his old county in fast time and Surrey won by four wickets. Shrewsbury received about £300.

His best innings of the summer came against Yorkshire at Trent Bridge: 'As ever he played all the bowling, on a not very easy wicket, with consummate ease' making 128 out of 335. Once more he was top of the Notts Championship averages. Topsy Wass, the fast leg break bowler, had developed splendidly and took over 100 wickets, Dick Attewell was finally pensioned off and young Jack Gunn supported Wass to the extent that the county rose fo fifth place in the table.

Shrewsbury was moving behind the scenes to secure the services of the medium paced Hallam from Lancashire and, using his influence, he obtained a job for Hallam in the lace trade in the winter of 1900/01. The capture of Hallam, who was a Notts-born man, proved of great benefit to the county over the next few summers.

The firm of Shaw and Shrewsbury continued to flourish, but relations between the two men were not very amicable. It is not known what provoked Shaw into writing to Shrewsbury and the copy of Shaw's letter is not extant, but Shrewsbury's reply is self-explanatory:

Sir,
    Your letter of the 16th to hand. When I tell you I am not surprised at its contents, knowing the vulgarity and little mindedness of the party writing it, I am only speaking what is true.

Whether to consign it to the waste paper basket as beneath my notice, or to acknowledge it in any way, took some consideration. This was the kind of letter one would expect from an ungrateful, malicious, disappointed man.

Now as regards the management of the business and the part I have taken in this, I am more than satisfied, and your opinion, whether good or bad, is equally valueless, as had I this, I should lose the respect and esteem of those people whose good wishes I prize.

I will briefly enumerate what my management has done for the business and at the same time the personal sacrifices I have made to keep it on its legs. In the first place for eleven years I never had one penny out of the firm, for the next eight years I had 30/- and from Sep 9/99 £3 per week. At one time it became imperative that fresh capital should be forthcoming, or failing that, the business would have to be wound up. I, not you, found that capital to the extent, with borrowed money, of between £700 and £800. Your sympathy and your duty to the business was practically demonstrated by investing what cash you had in gold and silver mines abroad.

So as far as you were concerned and by the help you gave, the business was doomed. Certainly I had 5 per cent for the investment, 50 per cent would not have recompensed me for the risk incurred. Some time after that period, and when it became necessary to purchase wood and stock for the coming summer, and an overdraft at the bank was absolutely necessary, I again, and not you, had to deposit personal security for £800, and I again, and not you, was responsible for that amount. Your practicability, usefulness, and duty to the business consisted in taking a back seat, or getting out of the way on these occasions. So by me and not by you a second time disaster was averted.

Since my return from Australia the latter end of 1888, I have paid off roughly speaking, between £3,000 and £4,000, the indebtedness of the firm at that time, and a little later. As regards the foreign wholesale trade, in every case, as far as I know, that trade was obtained by my efforts and my efforts alone. Adelaide, Melbourne, Queensland, Western Australia, Tasmania, New Zealand, Ceylon and The Cape of Good Hope, in all these places I opened accounts, and in some cases with several firms in one place, and in most instances these accounts are running now. These facts you are well aware of and they speak for themselves. Now we will try and compare – if it be possible to make a comparison – the magnificent services you have rendered to the business. As you are no doubt aware this was commenced in 1880 and except for an occasional and irregular visit, you took no practical part in it for about twelve years. I am aware you visited the place for a month or so at times during the winter and that was all. Not at all a bad record for the man who complains of those who have done the work, not doing their duty, whilst he himself, for over one half of the time the firm has been in existence, has done nothing, absolutely nothing, and has been practically an absentee.

If it was not for the audacity and impudence connected with such a suggestion, it would be almost too silly to be treated seriously. If again on the other hand, you are trying to play a game of bully or bounce, then it can only end in one way and that way spells disaster. Even when residing in the Meadows for a number of years, you only visited the place when you happened to be passing that way, and then only for a few minutes. That was I suppose the way you had of doing your duty to the business.

I have a vivid recollection on my return from abroad in 1888 of the serious position the firm was in, almost at the door of the Bankruptcy Court, and that despite the fact that it had had the advantage of your superior management during the whole or greater part of the winter. You had certainly during that period left an indelible mark of that keen preconception of business matters which you appear to credit yourself with, by summarily discharging an employee, who was under a three or six months notice, on the ground of incompetency, and the next moment so to speak, gave him an excellent all round character, one of his qualities was that he was thoroughly competent. The Law-suit that followed cost the firm between £30 and £40.

Another instance of your keen insight and shrewdness is afforded by the part of your signing an important paper presented to you by Mr Derbyshire, leaving it to him to fill in the whole of the writing afterwards. This was the only time you were left in charge, and you made two of the most egregious and foolish blunders it is possible to conceive. The above two instances are a fair sample of your management and I think not to be enlarged upon. To come to a later period was your arrangement with Fitchett re the stone turning.

If this was the best you are capable of doing, then all I can say is the sooner you control your own business, and not one I have an interest in, the better it will be.

Whether frightening a few mice away or using a sweeping brush, which is the work of the shop boy, balance the services I have rendered is too absurd to ask. I am perfectly satisfied with my share, and greatly disappointed with yours. I never heard any complaints of rats and mice being about when I foolishly allowed you to draw for 21 years £3 per week, and myself 30/- and I don't suppose I ever should, had I allowed that state of things to continue. Nothing you could say at that time was too lavish or too fulsome in my praise. I can see through all this now. As stated before I never drew one copper from the business for eleven years and yet I allowed you for the short time you had come to the place, to receive double the weekly payment I received, which you had never earned and was not entitled to. I most readily admit a very decided weakness over this transaction which I will promise you is not likely to be repeated. You never enquired whether I was starving for eleven years.

Your financial position away from the business did not concern me and whatever that position was, it did not entitle you to one penny more than myself out of the business. It was I and not you that was entitled to the higher wage.

My management of my business affairs during my life time has placed me in a position I am proud of, your management during your life time has placed you at the close of it, in a disappointing one, and that despite numerous and lucrative engagements.

I beg to remain, yours truly,
Arthur Shrewsbury

P.S. Referring to another matter, I shall be glad to receive a fair offer for my share in the business – I am aware of your estimate of its value, so that you may be relieved of my management once and for all. I am anxious to get out and any reasonable offer I shall be pleased to consider.

The quarrel was somehow resolved – there are no more letters to Shaw in Shrewsbury's copy-book. Shaw was in no position to buy out Shrewsbury and therefore must have apologised.

Another letter written in October 1900, but with the first

lines missing in the copy-book, makes Shrewsbury's opinion clear in a cricketing matter:

> You may always take it for granted the Australians will be over here as often as they think they can make it pay (they were due to tour in 1902). I don't, and never have done, blame them for this money grabbing, or for the Esq business and getting money under false pretences; the parties who are responsible for this are the Cricket Authorities in England, and more especially the MCC. Am sending you a little cocoa for a trial, please make it exactly as directed and you will find it cannot be beaten. To make it perfect it must be made with milk not cream. Let me know your opinion later ... We shall make a start in the large room on the Bridges (Trent Bridge indoor nets) in a short time, not exactly for the cricket alone, but more for the purpose of exercise.

The question of the lbw law and the excessive use of pads as a means of stopping the ball continued to exercise the minds of the MCC. Shrewsbury made the following comments in a letter to J. A. Dixon: 'If the alteration in the Law was made, it would in my opinion make the game slower and more uninteresting than at present, as on a sticky or bad wicket a batsman would simply wait for the ball breaking back, and play it should it do so, declining to run any risks by stepping across, and making a bona fide attempt to score, as the ball might come back and hit him on the leg. I remember some years back G. Lohmann speaking to me on the subject – he was at that time dead against any alteration, what his opinion is now I don't know – and he remarked that on a bad wicket a batsman could play with their legs, or in any way they liked, a good bowler would have no difficulty in getting them out, and on a plumb wicket leg play is not necessary. The new rule would affect many players who now play with their legs, who, if they know more about it, could with equal safety, use the bat. Again you find this class of player stopping balls with their legs, which would be inches off the wicket if left alone. It is this blundering kind of leg play which disgusts the spectators, who take it for granted that in all cases where the leg is used, the ball would have hit the wicket.'

The MCC called together a meeting of umpires to discuss the problem in November 1900. Shrewsbury wrote to W. A. J. West: 'Alfred Shaw thought the meeting at Lord's rather a tame affair, inclined to meanness. Mr Lacey's policy (Lacey was MCC Secretary) is tending rather too much in that direction, except of course the eye looks in the direction of self. My own opinion is that he merely made a make-shift of all of you, he simply had you there so that you could educate him in matters he was ignorant about, so that when he met his committee he could of course speak with some degree of authority. You were giving him a few wrinkles and at the same time paying for the privilege. It don't appear that any of you had sufficient courage to ask for out-of-pocket expenses, and as umpires of to-day are placed on a high social pedestal – much above ordinary pro cricketers – Mr Lacey didn't care to offend their sense of dignity by enquiring into such sordid matters ...' Shrewsbury obviously regarded the hierarchy of the MCC in the same light as he had the Notts Committee twenty years ago, when he instigated the strike.

Shrewsbury played for the County Eleven against the Colts at Easter 1901, but did not bother with the first first-class match against MCC. However the initial Championship game saw him opening the innings with A. O. Jones. Through May and June, Shrewsbury struggled to get runs and there was talk that he had lost his touch and would be wise to retire. His return to form occurred in the match between Notts and the South Africans. Notts batted second and were dismissed for 96, a deficit of 69. The tourists, through Shalders and Bisset, increased their lead by another 278, which left the county wanting 348 to win. By the close of the second day Notts second innings total had dwindled to 122 for 5. On the last day Shrewsbury scored an excellent 85, which though it did not save the game, saved some embarrassed faces. In the following match the veteran hit 99, and with his old partner William Gunn added 245 for the fifth wicket. This was against Derbyshire; then came 167 not out off the Gloucester attack and any thought of standing down from the side was forgotten. His change of luck coincided with moving down the batting order and allowing a promising young colt, James Iremonger, to open with A. O. Jones. This was the beginning of a most successful partnership. By the summer's end, Shrewsbury had completed 1,000 runs and averaged over 35, but from his county's viewpoint the important message from the year's work was that the creation of the ground-staff was at last paying. Iremonger and John Gunn made a great difference to the team's prospects, and with Hallam coming from Lancashire hopes were higher than at any time over the last fifteen years.

John Gunn did well enough to earn a place in MacLaren's side to Australia during the winter of 1901/2. Shrewsbury commented in the middle of the tour: 'I see the English Team are not doing very well on your side, and should they win another Test Match, it will greatly surprise me. Had Jones – the Australian – been in the same form with the ball as when last over here, I think the result of the tour would have been more disastrous than it will otherwise be. His falling off materially strengthens our side. The Australians will of course have to meet a greatly improved side when here in the coming summer, which if they beat, they will get full credit for.'

Shrewsbury predicted correctly – MacLaren's Team won the first Test and lost the next four. The two Notts representatives, John Gunn and A. O. Jones, achieved very little and the English side was handicapped by S. F. Barnes' injury.

Two other members of the party caused Shrewsbury a little bother. The two Warwickshire men Quaife and Dick Lilley had set up a sports business in Birmingham and were trying to test the water of the Australian market in between matches. Shrewsbury was informed of this by one of his Australian customers and replied: 'The reason Quaife and Lilley called upon you is that a clerk, who was formerly in our employment, is now working for them and of course he would tell them to do so. I don't think they manufacture, or if so, it is to a very limited extent.' The employee was Clarke.

10 Triumph and Tragedy

In the winter of 1901/2, Shrewsbury found himself homeless. The Queen's Hotel, his base since his schooldays, finally passed out of the family. Arthur had seen four landlords come and go. His brother William, who took up the licence from his father in 1885, had moved to 14 Cecil Street in Lenton in 1893. His sister Amelia, who had become widowed, married a local butcher, Josiah Love in 1888, and he moved from his shop in Arkwright Street, to become the new landlord of the Queen's. In 1900, however, the Loves retired to The Limes, Station Road, Gedling, and Albert Whitehead, Amelia's son-in-law (he had married Louise Vasseur), assumed the licence. His occupation was to last only eighteen months.

Arthur moved nearer the Cricket Ground, to 45 Trent Boulevard, West Bridgford, the home of his youngest sister, Mrs Louise Dufrene, also a widow. Altogether the Shrewsbury sisters had a most unfortunate experience with husbands, for Arthur's eldest sister was also a widow, having had two husbands. Her first had been Albert Radford, by whom she had had two sons, Albert and Joseph, and her second, married in 1884, was Charles Chapman, by whom she had a third son Arthur Edward, born in 1885. Mrs Chapman and her son lived across the Trent from Mrs Dufrene, at 48 Sneinton Boulevard.

Despite this change of home, Shrewsbury was still occupied in trying to expand the business. In February 1902 he wrote to J. S. Bowbanks in Montreal asking if the latter would be interested in acting as an agent for Shaw and Shrewsbury in Canada. His winter routine of visiting the indoor nets at Trent Bridge continued twice a week until the end of March, his main companions being his nephew, Albert Radford, his brother William, Walter Marshall, who had been appointed Notts coach in 1897, Neddy Briggs, the Lenton cricketer and young Snaith. Snaith was briefly a popular novelist and a very good club cricketer. He became mentally unstable, and living near the Trent Bridge Ground, used to harangue spectators on the way to the cricket with strange religious sermons from his bedroom window.

The Easter Colts Trial was a miserable affair on a wet wicket played on 21 and 22 April, but Shrewsbury turned out and made the highest score – 27 not out – when rain brought the match to a close. Nottinghamshire was the first County Championship side to play the 1902 Australians, this also being the opening first-class game at Trent Bridge. Shrewsbury was the only one of the twenty-two participants who had taken part in the very first Australian match twenty-four years before. He seemed quite determined to mark the occasion: 'Shrewsbury, after taking twenty minutes to play himself in before he had made his first run, gave an exhibition of the game which was almost worthy of his best days; he made most of his runs very slowly, but showed all the gracefulness of style for which he has always been so famous.' Shrewsbury made 73, but Joe Darling, with the aid of several dropped catches, hit a hundred for the Australians, who won the game by an innings. It was the beginning of a quite splendid tour, a personal triumph for Victor Trumper, and a galaxy of all-round talent, led by Warwick Armstrong and Monty Noble.

The Test match battles however were not for Shrewsbury. His efforts were entirely confined to county matches and despite the rain which marred the first half of the summer, Shrewsbury rarely failed. Ashley-Cooper, commenting after the first Test, played during the final three days of May, noted: 'The collapse at the opening of the England innings was not surprising. To say it was to be expected would be to invite scornful retort. The batsmen on the side were too brilliant a set to be reliable, and a steady bat such as Abel or Shrewsbury to have opened the innings with MacLaren or

Fry was what was required.' The first four in the England batting order were MacLaren, Fry, Ranjitsinhji and F. S. Jackson.

The reports of Shrewsbury's innings through the season are a repetition of his innings against Australia. One of the few feats that had eluded him during his long career was achieved against Gloucestershire in July. He scored a century in each innings – 101 and 127 not out. It was the first time this record had been performed by a Notts batsman and a collection was hurriedly taken and £10 quickly subscribed and presented to the veteran. The two innings moved him to the top of the batting averages, a position he was to retain for the remainder of the summer.

The Notts team improved during the last half of the season and were third in the Championship table. Tom Wass bowled quite excellently, his fast leg breaks taking 138 wickets at an average of 15·32, but the rest of the bowling was rather humdrum. John Gunn seemed quite stale from his winter in Australia and Hallam was only steady.

Wisden's Almanack devoted nearly a quarter of its review on 1902 Notts cricket to Shrewsbury: 'The batting honours of the season clearly rested with Shrewsbury, who seemed, as it were, to renew his youth. Far more even in form than in 1901, he was at his best when the season began and remained at his best so long as there was any work to be done. Scoring 1,153 runs with an average of 52 he had a record that would have done him credit in even his greatest days. Such a performance as his on the part of a man of forty-six has scarcely been surpassed except by W. G. Grace ... His batting was marked by all its old qualities, and except that he is, perhaps, less at home on a really sticky wicket than he used to be, there is little or no change to be noticed in his play. He was as patient and watchful as ever, and once or twice when runs had to be made in a hurry he surprised everybody by the freedom and vigour of his hitting. Whether he would have played for England in the Test matches if the Selection Committee had asked him we cannot say, but as he declined the MCC's invitation to take part in the Gentlemen v Players match at Lord's, he presumably does not care nowadays for anything more exacting than a county fixture. However as he is still both smart and sure at point he would have been quite in his place in the England eleven.'

The Notts Committee decided to raise an appeal for donations to a fund in recognition of Shrewsbury's batting in 1902 and £177 14s was given by his admirers.

Soon after the season ended – Shrewsbury's last game was for Lenton United v F. L. Browne's XI on the Gregory Ground at Lenton on 27 September – Shrewsbury complained of pains in his kidneys. During the winter he consulted various doctors, but to little effect, and the pain at one time grew so acute that he found difficulty in walking. In February 1903 he went to a nursing home in London for further medical examination, but the specialists could find nothing seriously wrong with him and he returned to Nottingham after a few days.

Instead of going to 45 Trent Boulevard, where he had lived for most of 1902, he went to stay at his sister Amelia's in Gedling. In the same month, he had a new will drawn up by his solicitors, Messrs Maple and McCraith. Mr McCraith was a noted local cricketer and in 1935 became the first Chairman of Nottinghamshire County Cricket Club.

During the spring of 1903, his health seemed to improve, but he did not feel well enough to go to the indoor nets at Trent Bridge and it was made clear in March, when he was unable to attend the meeting at which the 1902 subscription fund was to be presented to him, that it was very unlikely that he would play County cricket in 1903.

On 12 May he went into Nottingham itself and visited Jackson's, the gunsmiths on Church-Gate, where he purchased a revolver. A week later he returned to the shop, explaining that he had difficulty in loading the revolver. The shop assistant found that Shrewsbury had the wrong bullets for the gun and supplied the correct ones, loading the revolver with them. The same evening, at about eight o'clock, Shrewsbury went upstairs to his bedroom, asking his girl friend, Gertrude Scott, to make him a cup of cocoa. From the kitchen,

Miss Scott heard a sharp noise and shouted up the stairs to ask if anything was amiss, but Shrewsbury replied: 'Nothing'. A minute later she heard a distinct pistol shot and ran upstairs to find Shrewsbury bleeding from a wound in his head. Miss Scott rushed next door and fetched the neighbour, John Arnold, who came to the house and went up to Shrewsbury's bedroom. He stayed with the cricketer whilst Dr Knight of Carlton was summoned. By the time the doctor arrived Shrewsbury was dead. It was then discovered that he had first shot himself in the chest, but when that did not prove fatal, fired a second time at his head.

The inquest was held before a jury the following day – 20 May – in the Chesterfield Arms at Gedling, the coroner being Mr D. Whitingham. Only five witnesses were called. The first was Josiah Love, who explained that Shrewsbury had died at Love's house, The Limes, Station Road, Gedling, but that he was away from home at the time, the house being occupied by his wife, Amelia, Miss Gertrude Scott and Arthur Shrewsbury. Miss Scott was the second witness. She confirmed that she found Shrewsbury lying mortally wounded in his bedroom and that she went next door for help. She said that during the afternoon Shrewsbury had said, 'I shall be in the churchyard before many more days are up.' Miss Scott told him not to think of such a thing. Both the witnesses said that they were unaware that the cricketer possessed a revolver.

Three more witnesses were called, the neighbour, John Arnold, John Wigley of the gunsmiths and the doctor. Douglas McCraith, the solicitor, represented the relatives of the deceased. The coroner told the jury that the cause of death was quite clear and there was no disputing the fact that Arthur Shrewsbury took his own life, his mind being quite unhinged by the fact that he had an incurable disease. There was, however, no evidence to show that he suffered from any major illness.

On the morning of 20 May, the news of the death was telegrammed to the Notts team, who were playing against Sussex at Hove. As a mark of respect the match was immediately abandoned, and the last day's cricket was not played, the team returning to Nottingham.

The funeral took place two days after his death. It was the first decent summer's day of 1903. A large crowd gathered to watch the cortege make its way the quarter of a mile from the house to All Hallows Church, where the rector, the Hon. A. E. Bertie, conducted the service. There was a great number of wreaths, ranging from most elaborate ones from his fellow cricketers and the various County Clubs to those sent by the family. Among those present were J. A. Dixon, William Gunn, Alfred Shaw, Wilfred Flowers, Mordecai Sherwin, William Oscroft and Oliver Redgate, all being Notts cricketers, Arthur Paul of Lancashire, Louis Hall of Yorkshire. Shrewsbury's father, now aged 80, and his three brothers were the principal family mourners.

Arthur's suicide greatly shocked his father, who never really recovered from the blow and died eighteen months later.

There can be no doubt that during the winter of 1902/3, Shrewsbury decided to end his life. His suicide was no sudden impulse, indeed it would have been entirely out of character had it been so.

In the absence of any final letter, one is left to speculate concerning the reason for his drastic action. The obituary notice in Wisden's Almanack, written probably nine months after his death and therefore presumably after careful consideration, states: 'Illness which he could not be induced to believe curable, together with the knowledge that his career in the cricket field was over had quite unhinged his mind.'

The romantic view that he died because he could no longer play in county cricket does not in itself seem very plausible, especially when he several times writes in his letters of discontinuing first-class cricket and in 1888, he quite deliberately spent the whole of the English summer in Australia for purely financial reasons, thus missing a season at the very pinnacle of his career. In several letters he mentions how proud he is of the position he has obtained for himself in the world – not as a cricketer though, but as a businessman. The

impression gained by reading through his business correspondence is that he would be quite satisfied to live the life of
a successful businessman. At the time of his death there was
nothing amiss with the firm of Shaw and Shrewsbury – indeed, due to Shrewsbury's hard work over the previous ten
years, it was very prosperous. Shrewsbury had had quite a
number of difficulties thrust upon him not only by the managers he employed but by Shaw and Lillywhite. All these he
tackled and survived.

His suicide was therefore due to his acute hypochondria –
he uses the curious sentence, 'my health, as far as I know, is
all right', in one of his 1899 letters, as if he fears the worst
is only round the corner. In January 1903 his depression,
due to this imaginary illness, became very marked, but a few
months later he seems to have got over the most serious
stage. From being almost unable to walk, he journeyed the
four miles from Gedling to the centre of Nottingham alone,
but having made his mind up, he determined to go through
with his fatal action.

One can wonder why he did not marry Gertrude Scott,
who 'had kept company with him' for several years and in
one newspaper report is described as his fiancee. His feelings
for her are plainly demonstrated in his will, for she is the
main beneficiary, being left all his personal effects and
£1,000. Despite much research and appeals in the press, it
has so far proved impossible to locate anyone who personally
knew Miss Scott, so her feelings, even at secondhand, are
unknown.

Of his family, his sister Amelia, Mrs Love, was closest to
Arthur. On his voyages to Australia, most of the letters he
wrote to his family were addressed to her, and it was at her
house where he spent his last months. She received £400 in
his will, whereas his other two sisters received £200 each.
Mr Love died only a year or two after Arthur, and Amelia
moved back to the middle of Nottingham, to 7 Wellington
Circus. About 1919 she then moved to 7 Burford Road, off
The Forest, and remained there until she died in 1924.

Shrewsbury's share in the firm of Shaw and Shrewsbury

was divided between five of his relatives: his brother William, three of William's sons, namely William, Arthur Junior and Herbert, and his sister Mary Elizabeth's son, Albert Radford. Brother William moved to Fiskerton when Arthur's father died in 1904 and lived in Ebenezer House for the rest of his life, being looked after by his unmarried daughters, Florence and Mabel.

The running of the firm devolved principally on Arthur Junior and young William. The former, however, died of dropsy in 1917 at the early age of 43 – his career as a first-class cricketer had been confined to just three Notts matches in 1892, though he had also undertaken several engagements as a professional. Young William also did not outlive his father, dying in 1927 after several years' illness, and the business was then run by a much younger brother, Joseph, though two outsiders also acquired interests in the firm, firstly a Mr Bates of Epperstone and latterly a Mr Hunt, whose main business was in the printing industry. Soon after the outbreak of the Second World War, it was decided to close the firm down and its assets were bought by Grays of Cambridge. Joseph Shrewsbury then went to work for Redmayne and Todd's, a sports goods firm in Carrington Street, Nottingham, where he took charge of the cricket department. The premises used by Shaw and Shrewsbury have been demolished and the site completely redeveloped, so there is now no outward sign of the famous firm which for seventy years sent its cricket bats round the world.

Alfred Shaw died, also in Gedling, in 1907 at the age of 64 and like Shrewsbury is buried in the local churchyard, though not as tradition has it twenty-two yards from his former partner. Shaw, with the assistance of A. W. Pullin, published his autobiography in 1902, but despite his long association with Arthur Shrewsbury, he makes few references to the great batsman and none, save an advert, to the firm of Shaw and Shrewsbury. By 1902 the relationship between the two cricketers was none too cordial. They were contrasting characters, but two of the greatest cricketers who ever lived.

Appendix 1: Statistics

Note: All the details given are in accordance with the Guides to First-Class Cricket Matches published by the Association of Cricket Statisticians.

First-class Batting Averages Season-by-Season

	M	I	NO	Runs	HS	Avge	100s	50s	ct
1875	11	19	1	313	41	17·39	–	–	5
1876	15	28	5	603	118	26·21	1	2	3
1877	22	40	1	778	119	19·95	1	4	12
1878	24	39	5	724	74*	21·29	–	3	9
1879	15	24	1	363	87	15·78	–	1	10
1880	15	26	4	403	66*	18·31	–	1	14
1881	3	5	0	67	27	13·40	–	–	1
1881/2 (Aust)	7	12	2	382	82	38·20	–	3	8
1882	14	22	2	533	207	26·65	1	–	14
1883	24	40	2	1117	98	29·40	–	7	13
1884	20	34	2	908	209	28·38	2	2	18
1884/5 (Aust)	8	14	3	440	105*	40·00	1	2	12
1885	16	24	4	1130	224*	56·50	4	3	17
1886	24	38	5	1404	227*	42·55	3	8	24
1886/7 (Aust)	11	19	4	721	236	48·07	2	2	17
1887	17	23	2	1653	267	78·71	8	5	10
1887/8 (Aust)	8	14	1	766	232	58·92	2	2	14
1888	absent in Australia, managing football team								
1889	12	16	2	522	104	37·28	1	3	12
1890	25	43	5	1568	267	41·26	2	9	21
1891	17	25	3	1071	178	48·68	3	6	11
1892	22	34	4	1260	212	42·00	5	1	24
1893	25	43	4	1586	164	40·67	5	7	22

	M	I	NO	Runs	HS	Avge	100s	50s	ct
1894				did not play					
1895	10	18	1	647	143	38·06	2	2	5
1896	19	32	2	1009	172	33·63	2	3	12
1897	17	28	3	944	125	37·76	1	8	11
1898	20	34	7	1219	154*	45·15	3	7	9
1899	17	26	2	1257	175	52·37	4	7	9
1900	18	28	2	833	128	32·04	1	3	12
1901	19	33	4	1034	167*	35·66	1	7	13
1902	22	32	7	1250	127*	50·00	4	7	14
Total	498	813	90	26505	267	36·65	59	115	376

* not out

Test Career: Innings by Innings

			England's Total
1881/2			
1st Test	c Blackham b Evans	11	294
Melbourne	b Cooper	16	308
2nd Test	b Palmer	7	133
Sydney	c McDonnell b Garrett	22	232
3rd Test	c and b Boyle	82†	188
Sydney	c Boyle b Garrett	47†	134
4th Test	lbw b Palmer	1	309
Melbourne			
1884			
1st Test	b Boyle	43†	95
Old Trafford	b Palmer	25	180
2nd Test	st Blackham b Giffen	27	229
Lord's			
3rd Test	c Blackham b Midwinter	10	346
Kennington Oval	c Scott b Giffen	37†	85–2
1884/5 (captain in all five matches)			
1st Test	b Boyle	0	369
Adelaide	not out	26	67–2
2nd Test	c Worrall b Morris	72	401
Melbourne	not out	0	7–0
3rd Test	c and b Spofforth	18	133
Sydney	b Spofforth	24	207
4th Test	b Giffen	40	269
Sydney	c Bonnor b Spofforth	16	77
5th Test	not out	105†	386
Melbourne			
1886			
1st Test	b Spofforth	31	223
Old Trafford	c and b Giffen	4	107–6
2nd Test	c Bonnor b Trumble	164†	353
Lord's			
3rd Test	c Jones b Trumble	44	434
Kennington Oval			

1886/7 (captain in both matches)

1st Test	c McShane b Ferris	2	45
Sydney	b Ferris	29	184
2nd Test	b Turner	9	151
Sydney	b Turner	6	154

1887/8

| 1st Test | c Turner b Ferris | 44† | 113 |
| Sydney | b Ferris | 1 | 137 |

1890

1st Test	st Blackham b Ferris	4	173
Lord's	lbw b Ferris	13	137–3
2nd Test	c Trott b Turner	4	100
Kennington Oval	lbw b Ferris	9	95–8

1893

1st Test	c Blackham b Turner	106†	334
Lord's	b Giffen	81†	234–8d
2nd Test	c Graham b Giffen	66	483
Kennington Oval			
3rd Test	c Bruce b Giffen	12	243
Old Trafford	not out	19	118–4

† denotes highest scorer for England   * not out

Summary

	M	I	NO	Runs	HS	Avge	100s	50s	Position in averages
1881/2	4	7	0	186	82	26·57	–	1	5th
1884	3	5	0	142	43	28·40	–	–	3rd
1884/5	5	9	3	301	105*	50·20	1		2nd
1886	3	4	0	243	164	60·75	1	0	1st
1886/7	2	4	0	46	29	11·50	0	0	6th
1887/8	1	2	0	45	44	22·50	0	0	1st
1890	2	4	0	30	13	7·50	0	0	5th
1893	3	5	1	284	106	71·00	1	2	1st
Total	23	40	4	1277	164	35·47	3	4	

* not out

Of the matches in which Shrewsbury captained England five were won and two lost.

Shrewsbury was the first batsman to score over 1,000 runs in Test cricket and, discounting those who played in less than five Test matches, his average was the highest by any England batsman up to 1893.

His innings of 164 at Lord's in 1886 was the highest Test innings on that ground and remained a record until 1926, when W. Bardsley of Australia hit 193 not out.

Hundreds in First-class Cricket .

			Minutes	Fours
26 June 1876	118	Notts v Yorkshire (Trent Bridge)	210	13
10 May 1877	119	Players of North v Gents of South (Oval)	200	7
7 August 1882	207	Notts v Surrey (Oval)	395	24
26, 27 June 1884	209	Notts v Sussex (Hove)	390	31
5, 6 August 1884	127	Notts v Surrey (Oval)	255	18
23, 24 March 1885	105*	England v Australia (Melbourne)		
10, 11 July 1885	101	North v South (Old Trafford)		14
16, 17 July 1885	224*(a)	Notts v Middlesex (Lord's)	470	22
23, 24 July 1885	137	Notts v Gloucs (Trent Bridge)	405	15
24 August 1885	118	Notts v Derbyshire (Derby)	260	13
29, 30 July 1886	227*(a)	Notts v Gloucs (Moreton-in-Marsh)	465	15
15, 16 July 1886	127	Players v Gentlemen (Oval)	270	8
19, 20 July 1886	164	England v Australia (Lord's)	410	16
5, 7 March 1887	144	A. Shaw's Team v Victoria (Melbourne)		16
17, 18 March 1887	236	Non-Smokers v Smokers (E. Melbourne)		40
9 June 1887	119	Notts v Middlesex (Lord's)	255	15
13, 14 June 1887	152	England v MCC (Lord's)	315	15
30 June, 1 July 1887	130	Notts v Lancashire (Trent Bridge)	285	14
11, 12 July 1887	111	Players v Gentlemen (Lord's)	250	12
21, 22 July 1887	101	Notts v Sussex (Hove)	180	
8, 9 August 1887	119	Notts v Gloucs (Clifton)		5
15, 16 August 1887	267	Notts v Middlesex (Trent Bridge)	610	26
25, 26 August 1887	135	Notts v Sussex (Trent Bridge)	315	9
16, 17, 19 December 1887	232	A. Shrewsbury's Team v Victoria (Melbourne)	420	
10, 12, 13 March 1888	206	A. Shrewsbury's Team v Australia (Sydney)		
20 May 1889	104	Notts v Sussex (Trent Bridge)	180	8

Date	Score	Match	Minutes	Fours
15, 16 May 1890	267	Notts v Sussex (Trent Bridge)	535	19
23 June 1890	117	Notts v Lancashire (Trent Bridge)	310	
10, 11 July 1891	165	Notts v Sussex (Hove)	250	18
21, 22 July 1891	151*(a)	M. Sherwin's XI v L. Hall's XI (Bradford)	320	
20, 21 August 1891	178	Notts v Kent (Trent Bridge)	465	7
20, 21 June 1892	212	Notts v Middlesex (Lord's)	510	17
11 July 1892	151*(a)	Players v Gentlemen (Oval)	305	15
14, 15 July 1892	116	Notts v Yorkshire (Trent Bridge)	285	10
4 August 1892	111*(a)	Notts v Kent (Canterbury)	270	
15 August 1892	127	Notts v Gloucs (Cheltenham)	255	
8, 9 June 1893	164	Notts v Sussex (Hove)	315	22
15 June 1893	148	Notts v Lancashire (Trent Bridge)	225	14
17 July 1893	106	England v Australia (Lord's)	250	
10, 11 August 1893	124	Notts v Kent (Canterbury)	270	18
28 August 1893	101	Notts v Lancashire (Old Trafford)	255	
11 July 1895	143	Notts v Derbys (Trent Bridge)	260	19
16, 17 July 1895	111	Notts v Kent (Maidstone)		15
20, 21 July 1896	125*(a)	Notts v Gloucs (Trent Bridge)	315	
10, 11 August 1896	172	Notts v Kent (Trent Bridge)	410	
12 July 1897	125	Players v Gentlemen (Lord's)	220	19
24, 25 May 1898	154*	Notts v Sussex (Hove)	330	
16 June 1898	126	Notts v Sussex (Trent Bridge)	270	
12, 13 July 1898	103	Notts v Derbys (Derby)		
16, 17 May 1899	101*	Notts v Kent (Catford)		
8 June 1899	146	Notts v Gloucs (Bristol)	330	
13, 14 June 1899	114	Notts v Sussex (Hove)		
1, 2 August 1899	175	Notts v Yorkshire (Bradford)	330	
30, 31 July 1900	128	Notts v Yorkshire (Trent Bridge)	280	

			Minutes	Fours
18 July 1901	167*	Notts v Gloucs (Trent Bridge)	345	26
24, 25 June 1902	106*	Notts v Leics (Trent Bridge)	180	99
24 July 1902	101	Notts v Gloucs (Trent Bridge)	155	19
25, 26 July 1902	127*	ditto	215	19
11 August 1902	108	Notts v Derbys (Trent Bridge)	225	10

(a) denotes carried bat through the completed innings, which he also
achieved in the two following innings, though not scoring a hundred:

| 19 May 1890 | 54* | North v South (Lord's) | 140 | |
| 7, 8 July 1891 | 81* | Players v Gentlemen (Lord's) | 260 | 8 |

* not out

Notable Partnerships

1st wkt	391 with A. O. Jones	Notts v Gloucs (Bristol)	1899
	266 with A. E. Stoddart	England v MCC (Lord's)	1887
2nd wkt	398 with W. Gunn	Notts v Sussex (Trent Bridge)	1890
	312 with W. Gunn	Notts v Sussex (Hove)	1891
	289 with W. Barnes	Notts v Surrey (Oval)	1882
	274 with W. Gunn	Notts v Sussex (Hove)	1893
	232 with W. Gunn	Notts v Kent (Trent Bridge)	1891
	152 with W. Gunn	England v Australia (Lord's)	1893
3rd wkt	310 with W. Gunn	Non-Smokers v Smokers (E. Melbourne)	1886/7
	214 with W. Barnes	Notts v Middlesex (Trent Bridge)	1887
	137 with F. S. Jackson	England v Australia (Lord's)	1893
4th wkt	103 with A. Ward	England v Australia (Oval)	1893
5th wkt	266 with W. Gunn	Notts v Sussex (Hove)	1884
	161 with W. Barnes	England v Australia (Lord's)	1886
7th wkt	177 with Wm Attewell	Notts v Middlesex (Lord's)	1885

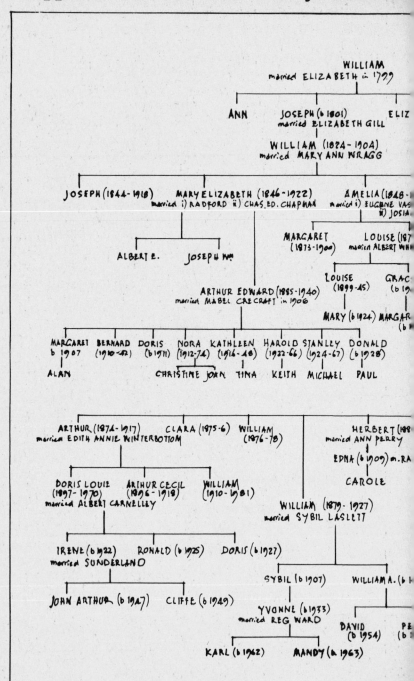

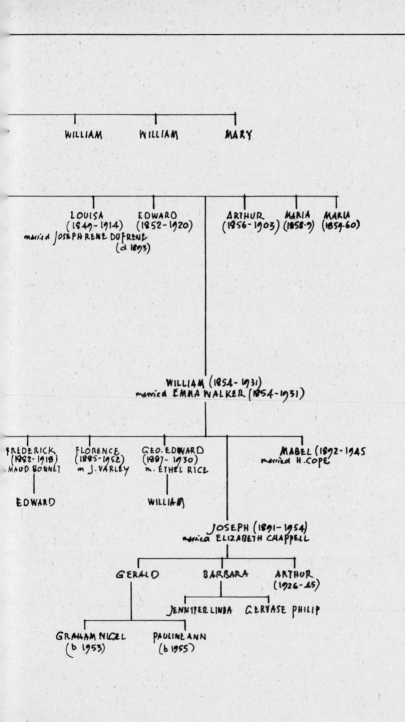